QuickBooks® Tips & Tricks

The Best of CPA911®

Kathy Ivens
and
Tom Barich

CPA911 Publishing, LLC
Jacksonville, FL

QuickBooks Tips & Tricks: The Best of CPA911

ISBN Number 10-digit: 1-932925-46-5 13-digit: 978-1-932925-46-3

Published by CPA911 Publishing, LLC July 2012

A Note to the Reader

From the Publisher

Although the tips & tricks found in this book have been updated using the latest version of QuickBooks (available at the time of this writing), they are applicable to most QuickBooks versions. Users of older versions may experience minor differences in steps and screenshots, but should have little difficulting utilizing the information.

Acknowledgments

Production: InfoDesign Services (www.infodesigning.com)

Indexing: After Words Editorial Services (www.aweditorial.com)

Table of Contents

Part III: QuickBooks Under the Hood   243

INTRODUCTION

This book is a compilation of frequently asked questions from readers of our books and newsletters, as well as from visitors to our web site - http://www.cpa911.com. Over the years we've seen patterns develop and decided that these questions provide a window into the areas that users most commonly need help with. Therefore, we have organized those questions, updated the answers using QuickBooks 2012, and put them in a form that will give users a quick reference to resolve many issues that cause confusion for both beginners and experienced users.

To introduce each different topic we have included a brief excerpt related to the topic in question, from one of our currently published books. This provides an additional bit of information for the reader, as well as a glimpse inside our other highly acclaimed references.

Since we have updated all answers using QuickBooks 2012, there may be some discrepancies between the specifics included here, and what you will experience if you're using an older version of QuickBooks. This should not present a major problem, as most explanations and steps are easily followed in any QuickBooks version.

PART I

ACCOUNTS & ACCOUNTANTS

CHAPTER 1:

ACCOUNTANT - SPEAK

The labels Debit and Credit can be confusing because they don't follow the logic of your generally accepted definitions for those words. How can an asset be a debit, isn't debit a negative word?

These terms are used all over the world, and date back to the 1400's; so it's too late to try to change them. Just live with them.

The solution is to ignore your vocabulary skills (and your logic) and just memorize the rules and definitions. You'll be amazed at how fast you absorb the concepts once you've begun entering, or examining, business transactions. There are only two rules you have to memorize:

- *Debits on the left, Credits on the right.*
- *Assets and expenses are debits by default; liabilities, equity, and income are credits by default.*

–Excerpt from **Accounting Savvy for Business Owners**
by Phillip B. Goodman CPA (available at www.cpa911.com)

Translating QuickBooks-Speak : A Guide to QuickBooks Terminology

Quite a bit of the terminology QuickBooks uses on menus, dialogs and wizard windows needs translation. The phrases are created by people inside Intuit who have agreed among themselves what the words mean, but their concurrence on these terms doesn't always take the English language into consideration. They've created "insider jargon", which almost never works well when taken "outside." Anyone with a minimum understanding of the English language can make serious mistakes in QuickBooks by applying a logical interpretation of the words and phrases presented in the software.

Accountants and professional bookkeepers who train and support users need to look at the QuickBooks terminology they see on the screen with a fresh eye. Read it as if it were English, and forget that you know what it means in QuickBooks-Speak. That makes it easier to train users properly, and saves you the migraine you get trying to figure out why reports don't make sense.

We hear a lot of negative comments about users' skills and intelligence from accountants who encounter company files that are a mess. Au contraire; users who make mistakes because of the dichotomy between English as spoken by people, and English as turned into QuickBooks jargon, aren't stupid; instead, they're the ones who are literate and logical. They just need to learn a second language: QuickBooks-Speak.

In this article, we'll provide explanations for some of the more egregious examples of QuickBooks-Speak. We'll also present some suggestions for changing the current terminology. Most of these suggestions come from readers of our newsletter, who send us e-mail to explain why users make some of the common mistakes in QuickBooks.

Menu Commands for Transactions

New users, who apply logic to the commands they see on the QuickBooks menus, frequently enter transactions incorrectly.

Receiving Money from Customers

Some of the commands in the Customers menu (those that relate to receiving money from customers) aren't named thoughtfully. They are extremely easy to misinterpret if you understand English and have a logical mind.

Receive Payments

When users who haven't learned QuickBooks-Speak need to record money received from a customer, they almost always select the Receive Payments command when they want to post a transaction involving income, whether the transaction is a cash sale (a sale for which there isn't an existing invoice, such as a retail sale, or a collection of money at the time of service), or a receipt of an invoice payment. After all, the terminology describes the task "record money from customers" perfectly.

Because the Receive Payments command should only be used when payments for existing invoices arrive, using the command to record a direct sale creates a credit (against a non-existent invoice). This, in turn, creates a lot of billable time for accountants who have to clear up spurious credits that should have been posted as direct sales.

This command should be renamed from its current "insider jargon" to something that's understandable by users of the English language. Readers have suggested the following names:

- Receive Payments on Invoices
- Post Invoice Payments
- Enter Customer Invoice Payments
- Enter Invoice Payments from Customers

Several readers suggested that the command must include the word "Customer" because most people use the word "invoice" generically; that is, you have invoices you send customers and you have invoices you receive from vendors. While QuickBooks calls an invoice a customer-linked document, and calls a vendor-linked invoice a "bill", that's not a rule of the English language outside of the QuickBooks corporate offices.

Feel free to comment, or suggest another name, by writing to editor@cpa911.com.

Enter Sales Receipts

When we ask new users what they think the Enter Sales Receipt command is for, the most common responses are: "Printing a Receipt", and "I have no idea ."

Those answers are very logical; it's the QuickBooks terminology that isn't logical.

This command should be renamed from its current "insider jargon" to something that's understandable by users of the English language. Readers have suggested the following names:

- Enter Direct Sales
- Enter Cash Sales

Customers | Vendors | Employees | Banking | Reports

- Customer Center .... Ctrl+J
- Create Estimates
- Create Sales Orders
- Sales Order Fulfillment Worksheet
- Invoice for Time & Expenses
- Create Invoices .... Ctrl+I
- Create Batch Invoices
- Enter Sales Receipts
- Enter Statement Charges
- Create Statements...
- Assess Finance Charges
- Receive Payments
- Create Credit Memos/Refunds
- Lead Center
- Add Credit Card Processing
- Add Electronic Check Processing
- Link Payment Service to Company File
- Enter Time .... ▶
- Item List
- Change Item Prices

Many readers explained that "direct sales" is a common term in business for the scenario in which payment is obtained at the time of the sale instead of creating an invoice. Some readers said that training users to translate "Enter Sales Receipts" to "Enter Cash Sales" occasionally caused confusion because some users thought they couldn't use that command for sales paid with a check or a credit card

Feel free to comment, or suggest another name, by writing to editor@cpa911.com.

Paying Vendors

QuickBooks offers two methods for paying vendors:

- Enter the bill (using the Enter Bills command on the Vendors menu), and then enter the payment (using the Pay Bills command on the Vendors Menu).
- Write a direct check, using the Write Checks command on the Banking Menu.

Many (probably most) users depend on both methods: Enter vendor bills for those vendors who send bills that you won't be paying immediately or won't be paying in full. Use a direct check for vendors that don't send bills (such as rent payments, loan payments that have coupon books or are automatic deductions from their bank accounts, and other "non-billed" transactions).

The Pay Bills command on the Vendors menu meets the criteria for "common English usage Vs. QuickBooks-Speak" confusion. A user who wants to pay a vendor bill that hasn't been entered in the company file often selects this command. Luckily, the Pay Bills window doesn't display a bill, so there's no way for the user to enter an unintended vendor credit.

Vendors	Employees	Banking	Reports
Vendor Center			
Enter Bills			
Pay Bills			
Sales Tax	▶		
Create Purchase Orders			
Receive Items and Enter Bill			
Receive Items			
Enter Bill for Received Items			
Intuit EasySaver			
Inventory Activities	▶		
Print/E-file 1099s...			
Item List			

However, facing the lack of a bill listing, the user often can't figure out how to pay an unentered bill, and ends up using the bank register. Then, the user sends us (or an accountant) an e-mail asking how to assign an expense to a customer/job, or a class. They're even more confused if they're trying to pay for an inventory item (using the check register doesn't receive inventory).

The solution is to have a QuickBooks command for writing direct disbursement checks on the Vendors menu, because it would be unnatural for a user to think, "If I want to pay a vendor I should look on the Banking menu."

Setting Up Items

We receive many messages from users with one of the following complaints:

- "When I create an invoice, it shows up on the bank register as well as on accounts receivable. None of my sales are showing up in my Profit & Loss Report."
- "When I create a sales receipt, it shows up on the bank register twice, once as a minus number, canceling the amount. None of my sales are showing up in my Profit & Loss Report."

Accountants and professional bookkeepers tell us they run into this problem at many client sites.

What's happened, of course, is that the QuickBooks item is configured with a link to the bank account instead of an income account.

Here we have another event where logic and familiarity with the English language backfires. Most people (including people who don't use QuickBooks) think of "bank account" when they see the word Account. When they see the word Account on the Item setup window, they select the bank account. You can't argue with the logic, it makes sense. Watch users set up an item, and when they select a bank account in the Account field, ask why they selected that account from the drop down list of accounts. The answer is probably going to be, "Because that's my bank account."

This field should be renamed from its current "insider jargon" to something that works for users who apply a common, logical, interpretation. Readers have suggested the following labels:

- Post Sales To:
- Income Account
- Posting Account for Sales
- General Ledger Sales Account

Most readers who made these suggestions said that they'd used different terminology when training users to set up an item in QuickBooks. They report that using the words "Post" or "General Ledger" stopped the automatic association of the word "account" with the bank account. If the users didn't understand the meaning of "Post" or "General Ledger", they asked their accountants or bookkeepers, which is better than automatically selecting the bank account.

Feel free to comment, or suggest another label, by writing to editor@cpa911.com.

Installation Dialog Messages

We started translating QuickBooks-Speak into English in our installation instructions for QuickBooks 2006, and we've continued our translation services for installation articles for later versions. Here's what you have to know to install QuickBooks properly (especially on a network).

Database Manager Vs. Database Server Manager

The database manager is not the same program as the database server manager. However, the QuickBooks installation wizard windows, the installation guide that is packed in the box, and the online support documents frequently use one of those names when they mean the other.

The database manager is a software component that manages the database, and it's installed when you install QuickBooks on any computer. Armed with intelligence about the nature of the QuickBooks database, the database manager makes sure data that needs to be written to the database is correct and appropriate before permitting the write (to a user, "write" means "save"). Users actually "talk to" the database manager, and the database manager "talks to" the data file. All communication between the user and the data file takes place through the database manager.

There's no particular reason for QuickBooks to mention the database manager in any documentation aimed at users (although IT professionals may be interested in the topic because of a natural curiosity about all things geeky). You can't "get to" the database manager, it's just there, working invisibly (the geek terminology for this is "transparent to the user").

The database manager should really be renamed from its current "insider jargon" to something that's understandable by users of the English language. Readers have suggested the following names:

- File Manager
- Database Structure Component
- Company File Management System
- Company File Underpinning Software

Feel free to comment, or suggest another name, by writing to editor@ cpa911.com.

The database server manager is an application that manages access to all the company files on the datafile server when QuickBooks is used on a network. That's an oversimplification, because the database server manager is also installed in a single-computer installation of QuickBooks, but it doesn't have the same role in that scenario. What's important is the fact that this is not the same component as the database manager that manages the actual data entry for company files, even though there are plenty of instances in documents produced by QuickBooks where the terminology "database manager" is used to describe the database server manager.

When you're installing QuickBooks, the text on the wizard window for installing the database server manager uses the phrase "Company File Server." To most users with any experience with a network environment, the word "server" refers to a computer, not a software application. You should mentally substitute the phrase "database server manager software."

The database server manager should really be renamed from its current "insider jargon" to something that's understandable by users of the English language. Readers have suggested the following names:

- Network Access Manager
- User Access Manager
- Network File Manager

Feel free to comment, or suggest another name, by writing to editor@cpa911.com.

Multi-User Vs. Host Multi-User Access

These two phrases have totally different meanings, but QuickBooks messaging text frequently uses them interchangeably. The misuse of the terms occurs in the wizard windows you see during installation, as well as most of the documentation provided by QuickBooks, including articles on the Support web pages.

Neither phrase is well thought out in terms of the way users understand the English language, nor do these phrases recognize common user scenarios for the QuickBooks software.

Many businesses have a single computer running QuickBooks, but multiple users access QuickBooks on that computer. In that scenario, it's perfectly logical for users to think of their QuickBooks environment as a multi-user environment.

Multi-user is a "mode" that applies to a single company file. When a company file is open in multi-user mode, more than one user can work in the file simultaneously. In order to have multiple simultaneous users, you must have a network.

Host Multi-User Access is a command that sets up the QuickBooks software on a particular computer to serve as the datafile server for network users. If more than one computer on the network has this command activated, users encounter errors when they try to access a company file.

Note that the QuickBooks installation documentation, and the text on the Installation Interview window, can be confusing, because QuickBooks uses the term "Multi-User" when referring to the setup of a datafile server for a network installation of the software. Mentally substitute the phrase "multiple simultaneous users on a network" when you see that phrase.

The command "Host Multi-User Access" and all references to it in the QuickBooks installation wizard windows should really be renamed from its current "insider jargon" to something that's understandable by users of the English language. Readers have suggested the following names:

- Host Files for Network Users
- Central File Location for the Network
- Company Files Storage Computer

Feel free to comment, or suggest another name, by writing to editor@ cpa911.com.

Managing a Change of Entity

In a previous newsletter we asked for your opinion on a common problem: A business changes its type of entity. A proprietorship becomes an S-Corp, a C-Corp, or an LLC with multiple managers. An S-corp changes to a C-Corp. An LLC changes to a C-Corp. Do you create a new company file and use the old file for historical information (including tax returns)? Or do you keep the existing file and adjust the information (not just the legal stuff in the Company Info dialog, but also move existing equity amounts into new equity accounts that you set up to match the new entity)?

Most of you said that a new company file is required. Some of the messages we received were very specific: "You must create a new set of books. Think of it this way: the old entity is no longer valid, viable, whatever term you wish to use. It just ceases to exist. The new entity assumes all assets and liabilities of the old entity. In fact, the entity should open new bank accounts."

One CPA provided a detailed answer that offered information in the context of 'it depends on what you're changing from and to.

1. A change from a sole-proprietorship to any other entity requires a new set of books. The proprietorship historical data is now irrelevant to the new entity except for a single-member LLC (a single-member LLC is not recognized by the IRS as a separate person, therefore, a new set of books is not needed or required), and except for the assets and liabilities transferred to the new entity. The new entity is a separate person as defined by the Internal Revenue Code, and must get a new Employer Identification Number.

2. A C-Corp or an S-Corp is the same entity type. They are just taxed differently; therefore, a change from one to the other does not need or require a new set of books. There are changes that will have to be made to the Equity section of the chart of accounts. There are also tax basis issues to be considered but is not a part of this discussion.

3. A change from a multi-member LLC or a corporation to any other entity would require a new set of books and a new EIN."

However, most of the mail we received said that accountants have found that it is always cleaner, better, and easier to "audit" company activities if you start a new QuickBooks file.

For those of you who wrote to ask this question, our only answer can be that there seems to be no absolute rule that covers every circumstance. Consult with your accountant (and calling a tax attorney might be a good idea).

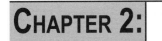

CHAPTER 2:

ACCOUNTANT'S COPY TIPS

An accountant's copy is a copy of a company file that's sent from the client to the accountant. The Accountant's Copy feature is designed to let the client continue to work in the company file at the same time the accountant is working in the Accountant's Copy, although there are limitations on the work that both the client and the accountant can perform.

When the accountant is finished working in the Accountant's Copy, the file is returned to the client so that the accountant's changes can be merged into the client's company file. Following is the process in chronological order:

1. *The client creates an accountant's copy of the company file and sets the dividing date (see the next section, Accountant's Copy Dividing Date). This file is the accountant's copy transfer file, which has a file extension .QBX.*

2. *The client sends the file to the accountant, either on removable media or by uploading the file to a secure server that QuickBooks provides.*

3. *The accountant opens the transfer file (.QBX) which is automatically saved as an accountant's copy working file, which has a file extension .QBA.*

4. *When the accountant finishes working on the file, the changes are exported into the accountant's copy changes file, which has a file extension .QBY, and the file is sent to the client.*

5. *The client opens the file and reviews the changes, then imports the data into the company file.*

–Excerpt from **Running QuickBooks 2012 Premier Editions** by Kathy Ivens and Tom Barich (available at www.cpa911.com)

Canceling an Accountant's Copy

When you create an Accountant's Copy, QuickBooks changes the attributes of the company file to prevent you from performing certain tasks until the accountant returns the file and you merge its contents into your company file. The title bar of your QuickBooks window displays a note that an accountant's copy exists as a reminder that you cannot perform certain tasks. (For a detailed list of what you can and cannot do, and what your accountant can and cannot do in the accountant's copy, see the Help files.)

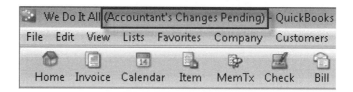

If your accountant tells you there were no changes, or if your accountant is unable to work on the file in a timely manner, you can change the attributes of your company file so it no longer limits your work.

Choose **File | Accountant's Review | Remove Restrictions** (Cancel Accountant's Copy in older versions). The message on the title bar disappears and you can now perform any task you wish in QuickBooks.

You cannot, however, import an accountant's copy from your accountant if one arrives by surprise. You must create a new accountant's copy and send it to your accountant. Fortunately, QuickBooks warns you about this before canceling the Accountant's Copy.

> **Remove Restrictions**
>
> ⚠ Doing this will remove the restrictions on your file that prevent you from editing transactions dated on or before 11/30/2011.
>
> **However,** if your accountant sends you a file of changes, you will **NOT** be able to import the changes into this QuickBooks file. You will need to get a listing of the changes and enter them manually.
>
> Please discuss this with your accountant before proceeding.
>
> ☐ Yes, I want to remove the Accountant's Copy restrictions.
>
> [OK] [Cancel] [Help]

Accountant's Copy Isn't Just for Accountants

Many business owners install QuickBooks in the office, and install another copy on their home computers, so they can work at home. They move the company file between the computers, by copying the file, creating a backup that's restored in each direction, or creating a QuickBooks Portable Company File.

Those methods all work, but the files are large, and, more important, what happens if the person who took the file home doesn't arrive at work on time? Or decides to take the day off? Anything the people back at the office do in QuickBooks is lost when the file comes back, is restored, and overwrites the current file. Or, it works the other way around; the changes made at home have to be re-created at the office because people have entered transactions, and you don't want to overwrite the file and lose the changes.

Use an Accountant's Copy instead. You can create an accountant's review copy of your company file, take it home, work on the file, and create a file to take back to the office to merge into the company file. Data entry takes place normally at the office, and when you merge the changes you made at home nobody's work is overwritten. To create an Accountant's Copy follow these steps:

1. Select **File | Accountant's Copy | Save File** from the menu bar to open the Save Accountant's Copy dialog.

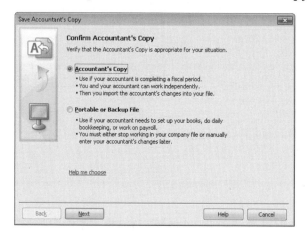

2. Select **Accountant's Copy** and click **Next**. QuickBooks offers a brief explanation of the dividing date and provides a drop down list from which to select the dividing date.

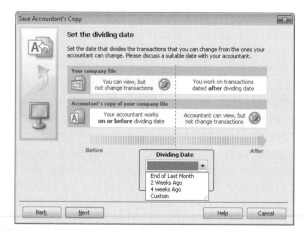

3. Choose the divididing date you want to use and click **Next** to open the Save Accountant's Copy dialog.

4. Select a location and file name (the default file name is fine for most users) and click **Save** to create the Accountant's copy.

If you're going to put it on a flash drive to take home, make that the destination. If not, remember where you saved it, so you can find it to take with you.

There are some limitations to the type of transactions you can create in an accountant's review copy, as well as some limitations to the type of transactions the office staff can create while an accountant's copy exists. However, most day-to-day transactions can continue while you wait to merge the changes. To learn what you can and cannot do while an accountant's copy exists, check the QuickBooks Help files.

Accountant's Copy Rules

Publisher's Note: This is the updated version of the earlier article which had been posted on the Intuit support site (with the permission of CPA911 Publishing).

This document contains information for the accountant and for the client about the work that can/cannot be performed while an Accountant's Copy exists.

Company File Compatibility

For the most accurate results, it's best that both the accountant and the client are working on the Accountant's Copy using QuickBooks versions from the same year. The accountant will, of course, be using the Premier Accountant Edition. The client may be using QuickBooks Pro or one of the Premier Editions. The accountant may work on an Accountant's Copy from one year prior also. In other words, if the accountant is running QuickBooks 2012 Premier Accountant, he or she can safely work on either a 2012 or a 2011 Pro or Premier company file.

Working on a company file from an older version (more than one year prior to the accountant's version) will probably not retain the changes made by the accountant.

Accountant's Copy – Accountant Activities

The work an accountant can perform in an Accountant's Copy is restricted as described in this document. The restrictions cover three types of tasks:

- Working with transactions
- Working with lists
- Account Reconciliation

Transactions

Accountants can work on transactions dated on or before the dividing date. However, to prevent conflicts with the work the client is doing after the dividing date, QuickBooks imposes some limitations to transaction activities. In addition, accountants can create some transactions that are dated after the dividing date.

For detailed information about what accountants can and cannot do with transactions, see the table labeled Accountant Transaction Activities, at the end of this section (the accountant's section) of this document.

> *NOTE: Be careful when preparing journal entries. Users have reported failures in importing the accountant's changes, and apparently quite a few failures are the result of a blank line within a journal entry.*

Lists

Generally, the accountant has restrictions on the work done with list elements that existed at the time the Accountant's Copy was created. However, the Chart of Accounts is an exception to most of the restrictions.

Accountants can create list elements for some lists while they work in the Accountant's Copy and for those newly created list elements, most restrictions are eliminated.

For detailed information about what accountants can and cannot do with lists, see the table labeled Accountant List Activities, at the end of this section (the accountant's section) of this document.

Reconciliation

In the Accountant's Copy, the accountant can reconcile accounts (bank and credit card) for any period that ends before the dividing date.

Usually, accountants perform reconciliation tasks for earlier periods because the client doesn't reconcile the account (preferring to have the accountant perform this task). In this case, the client should select a fairly recent dividing date (such as two or three weeks before the date of the Accountant's Copy) to avoid leaving the client's bank account in an unreconciled state for a month or more. Another solution is to ask for an Accountant's Copy more frequently, or have reconciliation performed at the client site monthly (perhaps sending a bookkeeper).

The accountant can reconcile periods ending after the dividing date, but those changes are not included in the file that's sent back to the client. The accountant can also undo reconciliations for any period, and if this occurs, the "undo" is passed into the client's company file.

Converting an Accountant's Copy to a Company File

The QuickBooks documentation on the Accountant's Copy feature includes the following information:

"If the restrictions on using an Accountant's Copy won't accommodate your situation, you can convert the copy to a regular company file. If you do this, however, your client will not be able to automatically import your changes. He or she will have to enter your changes manually in the company file."

In fact, this means an enormous amount of work for the client, because if you convert the Accountant's Copy to a regular company file, when you send the file back to the client your file overwrites the company file the client has been working in while the Accountant's Copy was out. At that point the client has two choices:

- Create a list of all work that was done by all users while the Accountant's Copy was out, and then import the accountant's file (and lose all the work done at the office while the Accountant's Copy was out). Then re-enter all the transactions performed by users.

- Get a list from the accountant of every task the accountant performed, cancel the Accountant's Copy without importing the file, and then create every transaction on the list the accountant provides.

If you have to do so much data entry that the restrictions on the Accountant's Copy get in your way, it's better to devise another solution. You should think about training your client to enter data in QuickBooks, or you should go to the client site to perform these tasks so you don't interfere in the client's ability to continue to create sales and pay bills.

Although you could warn your clients to stop working in the company file, because you'll be replacing it, this is onerous; your client won't be able to run the business properly until you return the file. And, if you have to do so much data entry that you need to convert the Accountant's Copy to a regular company file, it's unlikely you'll be able to complete all those tasks in a single day (or even a couple of days).

A good reason to convert an Accountant's Copy to a regular company file is because the client doesn't back up regularly and the company file has been lost due to a computer failure (or an inadvertent deletion of the file). In that case, in addition to returning a company file you've created from the Accountant's Copy, make sure you teach the client about the importance of backing up daily to remote media.

Accountant Transaction Activities

	On or before Dividing Date				After Dividing Date **			
	Add	Edit	Del	Void	Add	Edit	Del	Void
GENERAL JOURNAL ENTRIES								
Journal Entries	X	X	X	X	X	X	X	X
BANKING								
Write Checks	X	X	X	X	X	X	X	X
Make Deposits	X	X	X	X	X	X	X	X
Credit Card Charges	X	X	X	X	X	X	X	X
Credit Card Credits	X	X	X	X	X	X	X	X
Credit Card Refunds	X	X	X	X	X	X	X	X
Transfer Funds								
SALES & CUSTOMERS								
Sales Receipts	X	X	X	X	X	X	X	X
Invoices	X	X	X	X	X	X	X	X
Credit Memos	X	X	X	X	X	X	X	X
Statement Charges	X	X	X	X	X	X	X	X
Receive Payments	X	X	X		X	X	X	
PURCHASES & VENDORS								
Enter Bills	X	X	X	X	X	X	X	X
Vendor Credits	X		X		X		X	
Item Receipts	X		X		X		X	
Pay Bills	X	X	X	X	X	X	X	X
Pay Bills (credit card)	X		X		X		X	
Direct Deposit Payments			X	X				

	On or before Dividing Date				After Dividing Date **			
	Add	Edit	Del	Void	Add	Edit	Del	Void
Pay Sales Tax								
Adjust Qty/Value on hand (2011 and later - pre 2011 Qty only)	X		X		X		X	
Build Assemblies								
Payroll								
Enter Time								
Pay Employees								
Pay Payroll Liabilities								
YTD Adjustment								
Adjust Payroll Liabilities								
Adjust Liability Frequency								
Deposit Liability Refund								
Payroll Prior Payment								
Non-Posting								
Estimates								
Sales Orders								
Purchase orders								
Vehicle Mileage								
Pending Invoice								

** Edit, Delete, and Void actions are limited to transactions added by the accountant in the Accountant's Copy.

Accountant List Activities

LIST NAME	Pre-Existing List Element					List Element Created in Accountant's Copy				
	Edit	Del	Merge	Inactive		Add	Edit	Del	Merge	Inactive
Chart of Accounts	X	X		X		X	X	X	X	X
Class						X		X		
Customer						X	X	X		X
Vendor	X			X		X	X	X		X
Employee						X	X	X		X
Item	X			X		X	X	X		X
Fixed Asset Item						X	X	X		X
Price Level										
Sales Tax Code						X		X		
Other Names						X	X	X		X
Sales Rep										
Customer Type										
Vendor Type										
Job Type										
Terms										
Customer Message										
Payment Method										
Ship Via										
To Do										
Billing Rate Level										

Part I

	Pre-Existing List Element					List Element Created in Accountant's Copy				
	Edit	Del	Merge	Inactive		Add	Edit	Del	Merge	Inactive
Payroll Item										
Vehicle										
Memorized Transaction										
Reminders										
Alerts										
Workers Comp										

Accountant's Copy – Client Activities

While an Accountant's Copy exists, clients can work in the company file with certain restrictions, which are covered in this document. The restrictions cover three types of tasks:

- Working with transactions
- Working with lists
- Bank Reconciliation

Transactions

Clients can create, edit, and delete transactions dated after the dividing date. Clients cannot work on transactions that are dated on or before the dividing date. This means clients cannot create transactions with a date on or before the dividing date, and cannot edit or delete transactions that existed on or before the dividing date.

QuickBooks does not prevent you from opening a transaction that's dated on or before the dividing date, nor are you stopped if you make changes to any field in the transaction. When you close the transaction window, QuickBooks asks if you want to save the changes you made. If you select Yes QuickBooks displays a warning message.

When you click **OK**, you're returned to the transaction window. Close the window and select **No** when you're asked if you want to save your changes.

This restriction applies to any changes, including those that may seem unimportant to the accounting processes involved in a transaction, such as changing the text in the Memo field.

For detailed information about what clients can and cannot do with transactions, see the Table labeled Client Transaction Activities, at the end of this document.

Lists

The restrictions for working with list elements while an Accountant's Copy exists are not onerous. However, restrictions on the Chart of Accounts are a bit different from the restrictions on all other lists.

For the Chart of Accounts, the following rules apply (the term "existing" means that the account existed when the Accountant's Copy was created):

- Clients can create new accounts, and perform any action (edit, merge, inactivate, or delete) on those new accounts except create subaccounts.
- Clients cannot create new sub-accounts for existing accounts.
- Clients cannot edit, merge, delete, or make inactive existing accounts or subaccounts.

For all other lists, the following rules apply:

- Clients can add new list elements to any list.
- Clients can edit any list element.
- Clients can merge, delete, and inactivate newly created items.
- Clients can edit and inactivate existing items. However, if the accountant modifies the same item,

the accountant's changes will override the client's changes.

- Clients cannot delete a list element that existed at the time the Accountant's Copy was created.

- Clients cannot merge list elements that existed at the time the Accountant's Copy was created.

For detailed information about what clients can and cannot do with lists, see the Table labeled Client List Activities, at the end of this document.

Bank Reconciliation

QuickBooks permits clients to reconcile accounts (bank and credit card) while an Accountant's Copy exists, but when the reconciliation process starts, you see this message.

If your Accountant's Copy dividing date is only a few weeks before the current date, it's probable that some of the transactions in the bank statement are dated on or before the dividing date. In that case, wait until the Accountant's Copy has been returned and merged into your data file. The same is true if your accountant undoes a previous reconciliation (you'll have to contact the accountant to ascertain whether this occurred).

CHAPTER 3:

ACCOUNTS & SUBACCOUNTS

Subaccounts provide a way to post transactions more precisely, because you can pinpoint a subcategory. For example, if you create an expense account for insurance expenses, you may want to have subaccounts for vehicle insurance, liability insurance, equipment insurance, and so on.

When you have subaccounts in your chart of accounts, post transactions only to the subaccounts, never to the parent account.

When you create reports, QuickBooks displays the individual totals for the subaccounts, along with the grand total for the parent account. To create a subaccount, you must first create the parent account. If you're using numbered accounts, when you set up your main (parent) accounts, be sure to leave enough open numbers to be able to fit in all the subaccounts you'll need. If necessary, use more than five digits in your numbering scheme to make sure you have a logical hierarchy for your account structure.

When you view the chart of accounts, subaccounts appear under their parent accounts, and they're indented. When you view a subaccount in the drop-down list of the Account field in a transaction window, it appears with a colon between the parent account and the subaccount.

Because many of the fields in transaction windows are small, you may not be able to see the subaccount names without scrolling through the field. This can be annoying, and it's much easier to work if only the subaccount to which you post transactions is displayed.

That annoyance is cured by enabling the preference Show Lowest Subaccount Only, discussed earlier in this chapter. When you enable that option, you see only the last part of the subaccount in the transaction window, making it much easier to select the account you need.

–Excerpt from **Running QuickBooks 2012 Premier Editions**
by Kathy Ivens and Tom Barich (available at www.cpa911.com)

QuickBooks Subaccount Rules

We receive many questions from readers who are trying to figure out how to interpret the numbers they see on QuickBooks reports when they've created subaccounts. They complain that the arithmetic doesn't make sense, the reports are confusing, and nothing seems to be working properly. Most of the questions involve subaccounts of bank accounts, but the problems and solutions are the same no matter what type of account you want to track with subaccounts. There are rules to follow when you create and use subaccounts, and we'll explain them in this article.

When to Use Subaccounts

Create subaccounts in QuickBooks when you want to track transactions by a subcategory of a general ledger account.

For example, you have accounts for payroll liabilities and payroll expenses whether you do payroll in-house or have a payroll service. However, you can create subaccounts for each payroll liability and each payroll expense in order to track the individual liabilities and expenses in QuickBooks. These totals can be handy if you have to answer questions from a government agency about your remittances.

It's common for businesses to track categories via QuickBooks subaccounts for the Insurance Expense account (vehicle, liability, workers compensation, etc.), the Interest Expense account (loan interest, mortgage interest, credit card interest, etc.), and the Utilities Expense account (heat, electric, etc.). This makes it much easier to see subtotals if there's a question about these expenses.

For proprietorships and partnerships (including LLCs), it's a good idea to have a parent account for owner or partner capital and then create subaccounts for contributions and draws. You can see at a glance what the totals are for each type of transaction, which is better than looking at a net amount and then having to run QuickBooks reports to see the ins-and-outs of your equity transactions.

QuickBooks subaccounts of bank accounts make it easier to separate funds that require special treatment from funds that are available for day-to-day operations. For example, if you have a professional office that collects retainers from clients, or a business that requires up-front deposits from customers, those funds shouldn't be used for general operating expenses until you earn them. The solution is to use subaccounts to separate operating funds from customer/client funds.

Never Post to the Parent Account

When you have subaccounts in QuickBooks you only post transactions to the subaccounts; you never post any transaction to the parent account. Think about the meaning of that statement, because it means there's an inherent rule you must obey:

You can never create just one subaccount!!

Because of the rule forbidding you to post to the parent account, you have to create a subaccount for the category you thought you'd leave in the parent account.

Chart of Accounts		
Name	§	Type
◇ 100000 · Operating Account		Bank
◇ 100001 · Operating Funds		Bank
◇ 100002 · Retainers Held		Bank

Funding Bank Subaccounts

If the parent bank account already exists and has transactions, you have to create the subaccounts and then move funds out of the parent account into the appropriate subaccounts.

For example, let's say you decide to separate retainer funds from operating funds in your bank account to avoid spending down into retainer funds. (You don't need to open a separate bank account for retainers; that rule only applies to escrow accounts.)

You must create two subaccounts under the QuickBooks parent account: A subaccount for operating funds and a subaccount for retainers. The operating funds subaccount assumes the same role as a single bank account—it holds your operating funds. The retainer subaccount is where you deposit retainer fees, and then move the appropriate amounts to the operating subaccount as the retainers are earned and turned into income.

NOTE: *I'm assuming you set up a liability account for retainers or customer deposits as well as a QuickBooks Item that points to the liability account.*

You must know the total amount you're holding as retainer funds in your bank account. Technically, the amount you're holding as retainer funds is the current amount in the liability account you created for retainer funds. However, not all QuickBooks users do this properly; sometimes these records are kept outside of QuickBooks, in spreadsheets or on paper, instead of posting money received to a liability account. (Those users have higher accounting bills than users who follow good bookkeeping practices.)

When you have the total, you're ready to begin transferring money to your QuickBooks subaccounts. Create a journal entry to transfer the funds by choosing **Company | Make General Journal Entries**. In the Make General Journal Entries transaction window, credit (remove) the entire current balance of the parent bank account, and debit (add) the appropriate amounts for each subaccount.

NOTE: *Remember that this is a virtual exercise; the money is in your real bank account even though you are emptying that bank account of funds in order to fund the subaccounts.*

If you created more than two subaccounts because there are additional categories of funds you want to track, add those subaccounts and their balances to the journal entry.

Hereafter when you open the chart of accounts window, the balance displayed for the main bank account is the total of the balances in the subaccounts. The Balance Sheet (and reports on the bank account) display the balances of the subaccounts and the total for the parent account.

- If the total displayed for the parent account is not equal to the total of all subaccounts, you used the parent account for a transaction. Find the transaction and change the bank account to the appropriate subaccount.

- If reports on the parent account list a subaccount named Other in addition to listing the subaccounts you created, you used the parent account for a transaction. Find the transaction and change the bank account to the appropriate subaccount.

Depositing Transaction Funds into Subaccounts

Your company file configuration should specify the Undeposited Funds account as the default depository of monies. This means when you create transactions for received funds (customer payments of invoices, or cash receipts), the money is deposited into the Undeposited Funds account.

To deposit the funds in the bank use the Make Deposits feature. This is the best way to manage bank deposits; because it matches the way your bank statement reports deposits.

However, if you're using subaccounts you have to separate regular income from retainer income so the monies are deposited into the appropriate subaccount. First, select all the regular income and deposit that in the operating funds subaccount. Then select all the retainer receipts, and deposit them in the retainer funds subaccount.

Often, this isn't an easy task, because you can't tell which income is for regular earned income, and which is for retainer payments. The Payments to Deposit transaction window doesn't provide any clues about which receipts are for retainers, and which are for regular income.

The way to resolve this dilemma is to come up with a solution that announces itself in the Payments to Deposit window. Using the Memo field in a customer payment transaction window doesn't work, because memo text isn't displayed in this window.

Solve this problem with a new QuickBooks payment method, named Retainer, which you create using the following steps:

1. Choose **Lists | Customer & Vendor Profile Lists | Payment Method List** from the QuickBooks menu bar.
2. Press **CTRL-N** to open the New Payment Method dialog.
3. Name the new payment method **Retainer**.
4. Select the Payment Type **Other**.
5. Click **OK** to save the new payment method.

When retainers arrive, either as a payment against an invoice you sent for retainer funds, or as a sales receipt for retainer funds that arrived without an invoice, be sure the transaction window is marked with the Retainer payment type.

When you use the new Retainer payment method in Quick-Books transactions, the Payments to Deposit window is much easier to work with because the retainers are clearly discernible.

Depositing the receipts in the proper accounts requires the following steps:

1. Choose **Banking | Make Deposits** to display the Payments To Deposit window.

2. Select all the Retainer payments you deposited into the bank and click **OK**.

3. In the Make Deposits window select the Retainer Funds bank subaccount from the Deposit To drop down list.

4. Select the date on which you took the receipts to the bank.

5. Click **Save & New** to return to the Payments to Deposit window.

6. Click **Select All** to select the remaining (non retainer) receipts.

7. Click **OK**.

8. In the Make Deposits window select the Operating Funds bank subaccount from the Deposit To drop down list.

9. Click **Save & Close**.

You can automate the way you select payment types in the Payments to Deposit window, which is important in either of the following scenarios:

- You have a very large list of receipts in the window and you don't want to click off the retainer methods one at a time.

- You have other types of payment methods that have to be deposited separately (such as credit card payments which your bank handles separately on your statement).

To deposit different payment types in groups, use the following steps:

1. Click the arrow next to the View Payment Method Type field at the top of the Payments To Deposit window, and choose **Selected Types** from the drop-down list.

2. In the Selected Types dialog, choose **Other**.

3. Click **OK** to return to the Payments to Deposit window, where only your retainer payments are displayed.

Payments to Deposit

Select View
| View payment method type | Selected types ▼ | What are payment method views? |
| Sort payments by | Payment Method ▼ | |

Select Payments to Deposit

✓	Date	Time	Type	No.	Payment Method	Name	Amount
	12/07/2015		RCPT	35	Retainer	Bellevue Bistro:4th St...	500.00

0 of 1 payments selected for deposit   **Payments Subtotal**   0.00

Select All   Select None

OK   Cancel   Help

4. Select the retainer deposits you took to the bank and then click **OK** to open the Make Deposits window.

5. Select the Retainer Funds subaccount, and click **Save & New** to return to the Payments To Deposit window.

6. Deposit the remaining funds to the Operating Funds subaccount.

7. Click **Save & Close**.

Writing Checks from Subaccounts

When you create payments, be sure to select the appropriate subaccount in the Bank Account field of the transaction window. If you're entering a payment directly into the register, be sure to select the right QuickBooks subaccount. Usually, it's the operating funds subaccount that's used for payments, but the nature of your subaccount category (not retainers or another liability) may permit you to send payments directly from the appropriate subaccount.

Transferring Funds Between Subaccounts

When you invoice a retainer client you apply the retainer (or part of the retainer) to the invoice. At that point you've earned the money and can use it. If your subaccount(s) are tracking something other than retainers, when those funds become "spendable", that means the same thing: The funds are available for general operating costs.

To move funds from one QuickBooks subaccount to another, choose the **Transfer Funds** command from the Banking Menu and move the funds FROM the special subaccount TO the Operating Funds subaccount.

Reconciling Bank Accounts that have Subaccounts

When you reconcile the bank account, you're reconciling the parent account. Because your subaccounts are virtual bank accounts, instead of real separate bank accounts, the parent account actually maintains all the activity in the bank register.

Select the QuickBooks parent account for reconciliation, not a subaccount. After you fill out the Begin Reconciliation dialog and click **Continue**, the Bank Reconciliation window displays all the transactions for both accounts. In fact, the parent account doesn't pay any attention at all to the fact that there are subaccounts; this is just a regular bank reconciliation and no transaction shows any indication of being located in a subaccount.

Make QuickBooks Display Accounts by Number

A reader wrote to explain that he'd carefully planned the numbering system for his chart of accounts in QuickBooks, putting everything in the order in which he needed it. However, he doesn't know how to get the COA to display accounts according to his numbers; he wants the list to use his numerical order in every report and window.

QuickBooks sorts accounts by type first, and account number second. Therefore, you have to design your account numbers to match that order if you want to display the COA in numerical order. Here's the sort order:

- Assets
  - Bank
  - Accounts Receivable
  - Other Current Asset
  - Fixed Asset
  - Other Asset
- Liabilities
  - Accounts Payable
  - Credit Card
  - Other Current Liability
  - Long-Term Liability
- Equity
- Income

- Cost Of Goods Sold
- Expense
- Other Income
- Other Expense

Just keep in mind that QuickBooks will always ignore your account numbering scheme in favor of the account type. For example, if your liability accounts begin with 10000 and your asset accounts begin with 20000, Quick-Books will sort them by type, putting asset accounts (20000) at the head of the Chart of Accounts, followed by liability accounts (10000).

Subaccounts Named 'Other'

Several readers have written to ask why some reports are adding a subaccount named "Other" to parent accounts that already have subaccounts.

When you create subaccounts you should post transactions only to the subaccounts, never to the parent account. Then, when you create reports, QuickBooks displays the individual totals for the subaccounts, and displays the grand total for the parent account.

After you've been posting to the subaccounts, if you post a transaction to the parent account, QuickBooks reports that posting as "Other", to keep the parent- subaccount paradigm going.

Drill down by double-clicking the listing for "Other" and then double-click each transaction listing to open the original transaction window. Change the posting to a subaccount, and if you don't have an appropriate subaccount (which may be the reason you posted to the parent account), select **<Add New>** from the account drop-down list and create the subaccount you need.

Cleaning Out the Opening Bal Equity Account

Sigh! We receive many e-mails daily from users who don't know what the balance in the Opening Bal Equity account represents. Most of the e-mail includes the information that an accountant told them it would take time (which means money) to clear the account, or the accountant asked them what the account is for (accountants who aren't familiar with QuickBooks).

Amounts are posted to this account when you enter data into the Opening Balance field when you're setting up a new account in your chart of accounts (a balance sheet account) or you're setting up a new inventory item and fill in the fields for current quantity on hand and the value of that quantity.

To clean out this account you have to remember every transaction that went into that opening balance amount you entered when you set up the new account or inventory item. The number of users who can track that information is miniscule.

Never ever use those opening balance fields when you're setting up a new company file. Use real transactions. For complete instructions, see Chapter 1 of our book "Running QuickBooks 2012 Premier Editions" .

Hopefully, someday Intuit will listen to all the accountants and third-party book/article authors who understand how opening balances should be entered if you care about good accounting, and they'll get rid of the opening balance fields.

We heard a great definition of the Opening Bal Equity account from a CPA named Phoebe Roberts: "Don't set up any beginning balances (because the offset to each would be a garbage non-account called

"Opening Bal Equity," which in my opinion ought to be called "Quick-Books lacks an understanding of basic accounting principles"). It made all of us here laugh out loud.

CHAPTER 4:

ACCOUNTS RECEIVABLE TIPS

Accounts receivable is the accounting terminology for money owed to you, and it's often abbreviated as A/R. (In the business community, the common jargon for A/R is money on the street).

A/R increases when you deliver a service or a product and send an invoice to the customer, and the customer hasn't yet remitted payment. This is an asset because, as I explained in Chapter 1, an asset is something that you own or something that belongs to you, even if you don't have it in your possession at the moment.

NOTE: Some companies (usually retail businesses) never have an A/R balance because the customer always pays for purchases at the time the sale takes place. A/R postings take place whenever the amount of money owed to you changes:

- *A/R is debited (increased) when you create an invoice.*
- *A/R is credited (decreased) when you receive a payment on an invoice or issue a credit to a customer.*

–Excerpt from **Accounting Savvy for Business Owners**
by Phillip B. Goodman CPA (available at www.cpa911.com)

How to Write Off Unpaid QuickBooks Invoices

We frequently receive queries from users about the process involved in writing off old A/R balances. Some users want to create a credit with the date of the open invoice; other users ask whether they should use the current date. Some users ask whether they have to use the same item used on the original invoice.

For the question about dates, the rule is simple. NEVER enter a transaction dated in a previous tax year. Your books match your tax return so the numbers can't be changed.

For the question about the item to use, I prefer to create an item named Write-Off and link it to an Income account named Write-Offs or Prior Year Writeoffs (posting credits to this account produces a negative income total, and your accountant may prefer to make this account an Expense account).

The advantage of this is that it makes it easy to track and report on your write-offs. If you're writing off receivables that are several years old, the amount may be substantial. Since this lowers your net profit, your accountant (or the IRS) may want to know why this year's net profit is lower than previous years. The ability to isolate the write-offs (with an Item report or a report on the Write-offs Income account) makes what you did quite clear.

Chapter 4 • Accounts Receivable Tips **45**

Part I

After you create the credits, you have to use Receive Payments to apply the credits to the open invoices. If you don't, the old invoices will continue to appear on aging reports, even though the customer now has a zero balance.

Remember that write-offs are not the same as Bad Debts. If you file taxes on a cash basis, you don't have bad debts. Consult your accountant about the way to proceed before you decide to write off overdue amounts.

Understanding A/R Aging Categories

A reader wrote to find out why his accounts receivable aging reports seemed to be wrong. He explained that some invoice dates fell under the Current category, while invoices with more recent dates were listed as a month overdue. "I thought aging was a date-linked process", he said.

An aging report is a report on the invoices that are due, or overdue. If they're overdue, the A/R report shows you how overdue they are. However, the definition of "due" is dependent on the customer's terms.

A customer with terms of 60 days isn't going to be "overdue" 30 days after the invoice date, but a customer with terms of 10 days is. The only way all your invoices fit neatly into overdue categories (all the dates match the overdue periods) is if all your customers have the same terms.

Bad Debts

We often get queries about the way to handle outstanding customer balances that are clearly never going to be paid. Check with your accountant before you implement any "bad debt" processes (there are rules about this stuff), but here are the general guidelines.

Processing bad debt is a write-off process. If you file taxes on a Cash basis, just void the sale, because you didn't report it and therefore can't write it off. If you file taxes on an Accrual basis, you can use the following steps to write off the unpaid amount.

1. Open the Chart of Accounts and create an Expense account for bad debt (call it Bad Debt). Or, if your accountant prefers, create an Income account called Write-Off (postings to this account are negative income).

2. Create an Item of the Other Charge type, and call it BadDebt or WriteOff.

3. Link it to the account you created to track bad debt.

4. Create a credit memo for the customer. Use your Bad Debt item and enter the total amount that is due and deemed non-collectible. When QuickBooks asks how to handle the

credit, choose the option to leave it as an available credit (I find this preferable to applying the credit to the invoice, because it makes a better audit trail; additionally, it's also easier if the outstanding balance is from multiple invoices.)

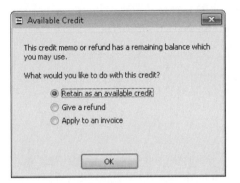

5. Open the Receive Payments transaction window. Select the customer, and leave the Amount field blank.

6. Click **Discount & Credits** to apply the credit. If there are multiple invoices, apply the appropriate amount to each invoice until you've used up the entire credit amount.

Discount and Credits				

Invoice

Customer:Job WeHaulIt Shipping Services:Software ...
Number   510   Amount Due   1,200.00
Date   05/08/2015   Discount Used   0.00
Original Amt. 1,200.00   Credits Used   1,200.00
                              Balance Due   0.00

| Discount | **Credits** |

Available Credits

✓	Date	Credit No.	Credit Amt.	Amt. To Use	Credit Balance
✓	12/08/2015	560	1,200.00	1,200.00	0.00
	Totals		1,200.00	1,200.00	0.00

Of all the credits issued to this customer, only unused credits applicable to this specific invoice are displayed above.   [Clear]

Separating Accounts Receivable by Divisions

A reader wants to know how to keep tabs on the aging and A/R data for wholesale customers separately from retail customers. He uses different transaction templates for each customer group and wants to have an efficient way to track A/R data. Classes don't work because balance sheet accounts don't have class-based reports.

The most efficient way to do this is to use two A/R accounts; one for wholesale and one for retail. QuickBooks lets you track invoice numbers by A/R account, so you can devise a numbering scheme that's specific to each type of customer (e.g. start the second A/R account with a six-digit invoice number).

You have to remember to select the right A/R account at the top of the Create Invoices transaction window, and you also have to select the right A/R account in the Receive Payments window (customer invoices won't show up unless the same A/R account is selected.

You could also use Customer Types to separate the customers, and then create memorized reports for all customer activities, based on the customer type.

Posting Rent Check for Sublets

A reader rents a large office space in an office building and has decided to sublet unused space to other businesses. He writes a monthly rent check to the building's management company and wants to know how to post the checks he receives from the two businesses that share the space. He doesn't issue invoices; the checks are just handed over to him.

There are two ways to do this, depending on whether you want to track the other businesses and their history in your sales reports and in the Customer Center.

To track the other businesses, create an item for Rent and make it a two-sided item. You can either configure both sides to post to the Rent expense (resulting in your net expense for rent appearing on the P & L) or post the income side to an Income account named Subleases. Use that item when you write the check for rent, and when you create a sales receipt to receive the rent.

If you don't want to track the other businesses as customers, you can skip the item configuration. When you receive the rent checks, use the Make Deposits window to enter them. Use the Rent expense account (to track net rent), or use an Income account named Subleases to track your rent and the income separately on the P & L.

Part I

CHAPTER 5:

BANKING TIPS & TRICKS

Business owners should always go over the bank statement and the bank register and compare them. Unlike the other reports discussed in this chapter, you don't view the bank statement to check figures and analyze them. Instead, this is a security check.

Unfortunately, statistics show that the rate of embezzlement in small businesses is much higher than you'd guess (and higher than embezzlement rates in large businesses). Even worse, a large percentage of embezzlers are family members who work in the family business.

According to a report from the Association of Certified Fraud Examiners, businesses lose 7% of their annual revenues to fraud, and small businesses are especially vulnerable. The median loss suffered by small businesses was estimated at $200,000 per business, which is higher, on average, than the amounts large companies lose.

According to the U.S. Chamber of Commerce, check tampering and fraudulent billing (the most common small business fraud schemes) destroy many small businesses. The American Management Association estimates that one-third of small business bankruptcies and at least twenty percent of business failures are due to employee theft.

–Excerpt from **Accounting Savvy for Business Owners**
by Phillip B. Goodman CPA (available at www.cpa911.com)

Reissue a Lost Check

A reader wrote asking *how to* re-issue a reimbursement check, in QuickBooks, that was given to an employee at the end of last year. The employee never cashed the check and has now notified him that she inadvertently threw the check away. This was an expense for last year and the tax return is finished. He doesn't want to void the old check in QuickBooks because that will change the P & L for last year.

The easiest way to do this is to write a manual check and use the date of the original check. Go into the bank register and change the check number of the old check to the number of the manual check. Then, to avoid having a "missing check number", enter a new check directly into the register with the old number and mark it void.

How to Use Virtual Checks

Every month we receive dozens of queries from users who don't know how to enter transactions that involve "virtual checks". Some samples:

"I use my bank's ACH services to pay vendor bills, but in the Pay Bills window I only have the option to write checks or use credit cards." "My credit card is paid in full with automatic withdrawals from my bank account. How do I enter the transaction with all the appropriate expense categories, since I can't use Write Checks because this isn't a check?". "How do I enter a purchase I made with a debit card, since it isn't a check?"

In every case, the transaction IS a check. Withdrawals from your bank account are checks. A physical check has a check number; all other checks (virtual checks) lack a check number but in bookkeeping, these are still checks.

When you use a virtual check (in the Write Checks window, the Pay Bills window, or directly in the bank account register) you can either leave the check number blank or use a "code" for the check (e.g. ACH, E-Check, DebitCard, etc.).

In the Pay Bills window be sure to select the **Assign Check Number** option so you can enter the desired code.

Then, when the Assign Check Nubers dialog opens, enter the code in the Check No. field.

The decision about using a code or not depends on the way your bank arranges your statement. Our bank account, for example, lists all physical checks first and then lists all electronic withdrawals in date order. To make it easier to reconcile the bank in QuickBooks, we leave check numbers blank for virtual checks. If your bank lists ACH transactions separately from Debit Card transactions, then using codes will make it easier to use the Reconcile window.

First Bank Reconciliation in QuickBooks

A reader wrote to say he'd entered the opening balance for his checking account in QuickBooks using a journal entry. When he opened the reconciliation window for the checking account, the screen shows that the beginning balance is $0. He tried changing the date of the journal entry to a month later than the original entry, but the beginning balance on the reconciliation window was still $0. He says that he's finding it impossible to reconcile his bank account.

The beginning balance you see in the QuickBooks reconciliation window shows you the beginning balance from the last reconciliation, not the balance of your bank register. For the first reconciliation, this would have to be zero. Reconcile the first month by selecting all the transactions that cleared for that month. The ending balance (which should match the ending balance on the statement for that month) will be the beginning balance of the next reconciliation, and so on and so on.

How to Modify a QuickBooks Bank Deposit

A reader wrote to explain that he'd opened a second bank account that is dedicated to receiving credit card deposits (the bank is his merchant bank and offers better fees if you open a bank account to receive the deposits). The deposits were erroneously deposited into his original bank account in QuickBooks. He wants to know how to change those deposits. The cash/check deposits were deposited separately into the original bank account.

The process is fairly simple:

1. Press **CTRL-R** to display the Use Register dialog box.
2. Select the bank account into which the erroneous deposits were made, and click **OK** to open the account register.

3. Right click the first erroneous deposit and choose **Edit Deposit** from the shortcut menu that appears. This opens the deposit in the Make Deposits window.

4. At the top of the Make Deposits window, select the *correct* bank account from the Deposit To drop down list.

5. Click **Save & Close** to return to the account register.

6. Repeat the process for each erroneous deposit.

How to Void a Previous Year's Check in QuickBooks

Many many readers ask this question: How can I void a check in QuickBooks that I wrote last year, that never cleared? One reader wrote recently to say his *accountant* said he can't change last year's numbers because his tax return used those numbers.

First of all, good for you for asking your accountant; because too many users just plunge in and do stuff without asking, and then have to pay their accountants more when the beginning numbers for the current tax year don't match the ending numbers from the previous tax year.

Instead of voiding a QuickBooks transaction from the previous year, enter a deposit using the current date. Use the same payee, the same amount, and the same expense account as the check you wanted to void. When you reconcile the bank account clear both the outstanding check and the deposit you created (since they "wash" they don't change the rec-onciled balance).

Debits on the Wrong Side in Bank Reconciliation?

A reader tells us that he finally memorized the mantra "debits on the left, credits on the right" so he could understand the instructions from his accountant when he creates journal entries. He went on to say that now that he has this firmly fixed in his brain he's noticed that the Bank

Reconciliation window has the debits and credits reversed. "My checks, which are credits, are on the left, and the deposits, which are debits, are on the right; did I memorize it backwards?"

The Bank Reconciliation feature is designed to follow the way your bank statements appear. To your bank, it's all the other way around. Money you deposit is a debit to you (it's an asset), but to the bank it's a liability (money the bank is holding for you). Over the years, we've had several employees who worked at banks before they came to work for us, and it took them a while to get used to the debit/credit paradigm in the accounting software we used and supported.

Clearing the Undeposited Funds Account

A reader wrote with the following problem: "My Undeposited Funds account has thousands of dollars in it, representing several months of deposits. I think the former bookkeeper (who worked here for only a few months) reconciled by adding transactions on the printed statement to the register if they weren't already there, instead of using the Make Deposits function.

Luckily, when she added the deposit to the register, she didn't put in a customer name. She didn't understand how to use the Undeposited Funds account. The customer payments are accurate, the bank balance is accurate, but the Income totals are too high and the Undeposited Funds total is showing up on our Balance Sheet. I can't figure out how to fix this."

Create a journal entry that credits the existing balance in the Undeposited Funds account and debits the Income account for the same amount.

Then go to the Make Deposits screen, where you'll see all the un-deposited transactions as well as the journal entry (which is a negative number equal to the total of all the transactions). Select **All** to create a zero amount deposit and clear all the entries. (If the bookkeeper had posted each transaction to the appropriate customer, you would have to void each of the duplicate customer transactions.)

Rename Undeposited Funds to Help Explain It

We receive tons of questions about the Undeposited Funds account, which many users don't understand. They don't understand why they see that account referenced in the bank register, or in reports. They don't understand why it's difficult to reconcile the bank account each month if they change the QuickBooks configuration so that money is deposited directly into a bank account instead of into the Undeposited Funds account.

As an experiment, we began telling some accountants to rename the account, to see if it helped users understand the account's role. They've reported that the "trick" worked, and many of their clients understood the function better (and stopped calling them with questions).

Here are some of the new names that accountants found "successful": "Take This to the Bank", "Money Not Yet Taken to The Bank", "Money Not Deposited in the Bank ", and "Money Awaiting a Bank Deposit."

Some people responded with, "But the title means Undeposited Funds", but other users found the new title helpful.

To change the name of the account:

1. Press **CTRL-A** to open the Chart of Accounts window
2. Select the Undeposited Funds account (it's an "Other Current Asset" account type).
3. Press **CTRL-E** to open the Edit Account dialog box.
4. Type the new name in the Account Name Field.
5. Click **Save & Close** to save the name change.

Transferring Funds Between Banks

A reader wrote to say he often transfers funds between his company's payroll account and the operating account, using a check. He needs to record the check number so it appears in the Check Number field of the bank register, and the Transfer Funds command on the Banking Menu doesn't provide a place to put the check number. He wants to know how to record a funds transfer in one step that will record the check number.

There is no one-step way to do this. Here are some alternative methods, which may or may not be satisfactory:

Use the Memo field in the Transfer Funds window to record the check number, which means no number appears in the Number field of the bank register (but you'll have the check number information you need).

After you use the Transfer Funds window, if you open the register of the account from which the check was written and enter the check number in the Number field, that change is replicated in the receiving account (which of course, did not use that check number for the transaction). Using the Transfer Funds window creates a "mirrored transaction" and whatever you alter in one account is echoed in the other account.

Use the Write Checks window and post the check to the receiving bank account instead of to an expense. However, the check number of the sending account appears in the Number column of the bank register of the receiving bank account, and you cannot delete it.

Create a new bank account called Funds Transfer. Use the Write Checks window and post the check to that new transfer account (creating a debit balance in the transfer account). Then bring the money into the receiving account (either using the account register or the Make Deposits window) using the transfer account as the source of the deposit (creating a credit that zeroes out the balance in the transfer account).

And finally, our favorite, if both accounts are in the same bank, use your bank's online banking features to transfer funds between accounts. When you record the transaction in QuickBooks, use EFT (Electronic Funds Transfer) in the Number field. This also means you saved the cost of the check, as well as a trip to the bank to deposit the check.

Check Recorded in Wrong Bank Account

A reader wanted to know how to move a check from one account to another. She manually wrote the check from the company's checking account, but then when she entered it in QuickBooks, she used the company's money market account by mistake.

This is one of those easy fixes that requires a minimal amount of effort, and no fancy footwork.

1. Press **CTRL-R** to display the Use Register dialog box.
2. Select the account to which the check was incorrectly posted (the money market account in our reader's example) to open the account register.
3. Right-click the check's listing.
4. From the shortcut menu that appears, select **Edit Check** to open the check window
5. Now, select the right account from the drop-down list in the Bank Account field at the top of the window.

6. Click **Save & Close** to accept the change.

QuickBooks will move the check to the right bank account.

Avoid Confusion With Multiple Bank Accounts

In our last newsletter we explained how to change the bank account that was used when a check was inadvertently created in the wrong account.

A QuickBooks consultant wrote to tell us that she has clients change the display of the color of the bank registers so they match the color of the physical checks.

To change the color displayed in the bank register, follow these steps:

1. Press **CTRL-R** to open the open the Use Register window.

2. Choose the account for which you want to change the register color.

3. From the QuickBooks menu bar, select **Edit | Change Account Color** to open the Change Color dialog/palette.

4. Select a color that matches or comes close to the color of the physical checks.

When you open the Write Checks window, the color of the check changes to match the color assigned to the register. Thanks to Quick-Books consultant Liz Fleming for this tip.

Memorized ACH Payments

A reader wrote to explain that she uses memorized transactions for monthly checks that are always for the same amount (such as rent). She has recently arranged to have some payments taken directly from the bank account. QuickBooks automatically inserts the next available check number, so when she creates the next physical check she's told the check number is already in use.

The fix is to enter ACH in the Check No. field of the memorized check in QuickBooks.

Tracking Transfers Between Banks

A reader couldn't figure out how to create a report that shows all the funds transferred between bank accounts.

1. Choose **Reports | Accountant & Taxes | Transaction Detail By Account**.
2. Select the Date Range you need.
3. Click **Customize Report** (Modify Report in pre-2012 versions).
4. Go to the Filters tab.
5. Select **Account** from the Choose Filter list, and then select **All Bank Accounts**.
6. Return to the Choose Filter list and select **Transaction Type** as the filter, and then select **Transfer**.

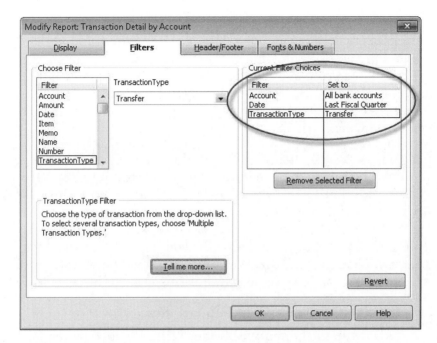

7. Click **OK** to view the funds transfer report.

Online Banking Functions Stop Working

Every year during the month of June we get deluged with readers asking for help with their online features (online banking, e-mail, merchant accounts, etc.).

The reason is that every year at the end of May, Intuit "sunsets' an earlier version of QuickBooks. In other words they stop supporting it and suspend all online functionality. Currently, Intuit will only support the four most recent versions. Therefore, in May of 2011, QuickBooks 2008 was "sunsetted", leaving QuickBooks 2009, 2010. 2011, and 2012 as the only versions supported (and with online functionality) by Intuit. Presumably, at the end of May 2012, QuickBooks 2009 will be sunsetted, and so on.

When a version is sunsetted, QuickBooks will continue to run, but no further updates to fix bugs will be released. More important, QuickBooks services that are accessed outside of the software will no longer work (online banking, payroll, merchant card services, QuickBooks e-mail, etc.). If you don't use any QuickBooks services, you can continue to work in the sunsetted version. If you need any of these services you have to update your version of QuickBooks.

If you choose to keep using a sunsetted version of QuickBooks you need to think about how to re-install it when your computer or hard drive dies (notice that I said "when", not "if"). Your original QuickBooks software CD is probably an earlier version than the version you were running, because you updated QuickBooks over the years. If you have to re-install the software, your company file won't open because it was saved with a later version. QuickBooks continues to provide manual updates for sunsetted products, or you can prepare for this eventuality yourself:

1. Go to the QuickBooks support site.
2. Download the manual update file. Be sure to choose **Save** in the Download dialog.
3. After the file is saved on your hard drive, burn the file to a CD. Label the CD "2xxx Rxx" (R being the release number) and put it away with your original QuickBooks software CD.

If you have to reinstall QuickBooks, run the downloaded file after you've finished installing the original CD. Then open your company file.

Removing a Check from a Deposit

A reader wrote that he'd used the Make Deposits window to deposit 11 checks. When he went to the bank he remembered that one of the checks was supposed to be held for a few days before depositing it. He deposited the other 10 checks, and wants to know how to correct the deposit total in QuickBooks.

1. Select **Banking | Make Deposits** to open the Make Deposits window.

2. Click the **Previous** button to find the deposit

3. Select the line with the check you didn't deposit and press **CTRL+DEL** (hold down the Ctrl key while you press the Delete key).

That check is removed from the deposit (and will be waiting for you the next time you open the Make Deposits window), and QuickBooks will re-calculate the amount of the deposit so you can reconcile the account at the end of the month.

Note: You could also open the account register, right-click the deposit listing, and select Edit Deposit.

Copying a Check

We've had queries from several readers about copying checks. They don't want to memorize the check, but occasionally a check goes out that's identical to a previous check (not necessarily the last check written to the vendor in question). They want to know if there's an easier way than opening a blank Write Checks window and filling in the check, because the check they want to duplicate has many line items.

There is a way to copy a check:

1. Press **CTRL-R** to display the Use Register dialog.

2. Select the check you want to copy. The transaction type must be CHK (this doesn't work with BILLPMT, TAXPMT LIAB CHK, or PAY CHK).

3. Press **CTRL-O** (the letter "O", not a zero) to copy the check.

4. Press **CTRL-V** to paste the check.

QuickBooks automatically puts the copied check on the line below the original check. Everything is exactly the same (including the date) except the check number (which is the next available check number for the bank account). Change the date and click **Record** to move the check to the proper place in the register.

Printing a List of Bank Deposits

A reader wrote to say that her employer wants a list of all bank deposits made for a given period, and she doesn't know how to produce the list.

1. Press **CTRL-A** to open the Chart of Accounts window.
2. Select (highlight) the bank account and press **CTRL-Q** to open a QuickReport of all transactions for the account.
3. Set the time period for the dates you need.
4. Click **Customize Report** (Modify Report in pre-2012 versions) and move to the Filters tab.
5. Select **Transaction Type** in the Choose Filter list.
6. Select **Deposit** as the Transaction Type.

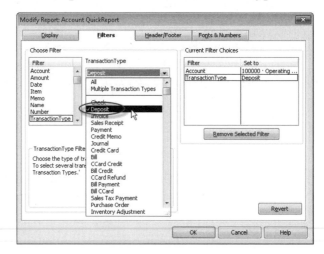

7. Click **OK**.

Memorize the report, naming it "List of Deposits" (or something similar) so you don't have to go through the configuration steps in the future.

Customer Funds Deposited Incorrectly

A reader wrote with the following question: "I just found a problem with one of my deposits from several months ago. There were six checks received and deposited all at once, using the Make Deposits window, and posting each check to the right income account. Now I realize that one of those checks was a customer invoice payment, not a direct sale. The customer shows an open balance. I can't find this customer's check in the Customer Center. If I have to remove the entire deposit and re-enter each check I received I'll have a problem because the deposit cleared and was reconciled. How do I fix this?"

This user has two things to fix: The incorrectly applied check, and the method he's using to record money received from customers.

To correct the incorrectly applied check, use the following steps:

1. Press **CTRL-R** to open the Use Register dialog.

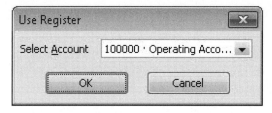

2. Select the appropriate account and click **OK** to open the account register.
3. Right-click the deposit in your bank register and choose **Edit Deposit** to open the Make Deposits window.
4. In the Make Deposits window, select the check in question and make sure the customer's name is in the Received From column.

5. In the From Account column, change the account to **Accounts Receivable**. This creates a credit for the customer named in the Received From column.

6. Click **Save & Close** to save the changed deposit. You haven't changed any amounts, so the deposit remains the same, and is still reconciled.

7. Choose **Customers | Receive Payments** from the menu bar to open the Receive Payments window.

8. From the Received From drop down list, choose the customer in question.

9. Apply the credit you just created to the invoice that has the open balance.

10. Click **Save & Close** to complete the procedure.

To track customer sales properly, stop using the Make Deposits window; instead, use the Sales Receipt transaction form for cash sales and Receive Payments for customer invoice payments.

While the Make Deposits window seems faster and more efficient, it has several serious drawbacks:

1. The transactions entered in the Make Deposits window don't appear in the customer's record in the Customer Center. This means you don't see an accurate history of any customer's activity.

2. The transactions entered in the Make Deposits window don't appear in standard Sales reports (reports available from Reports | Sales). This means your sales totals in those reports won't match the sales totals on your Profit & Loss statement, which will drive your accountant crazy.

3. You can't link to an item in the Make Deposits window, which means you lose some valuable reports when you analyze your business (this problem isn't important if you have only one item set up in your company file).

The reason the Make Deposits window doesn't work properly for sales is the way that function handles Source data and Target data. Customer transactions show up in the customer history and in sales reports when the customer is the "source" data, which is how it works in the Sales Receipt transaction form. In the Make Deposits window, the bank account is the Source data and the customer is the Target data.

Part I

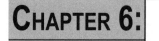

CHAPTER 6:

TIPS FOR CHARITABLE GIFTS

Charitable contributions made by a sole proprietorship are not deductible by the business, but are deductible by the proprietor as if made personally.

If you provide an inventory product to a nonprofit organization, use your Charitable Contributions expense account.

If your employees have contributions withheld for a charitable organization, you remit the donation periodically. Many businesses offer a matching amount to these withheld funds (or a partial match), and those matching funds are an expense (posted to Charitable Contributions).

–Excerpts from **Accounting Savvy for Business Owners**
by Phillip B. Goodman CPA (available at www.cpa911.com)

Gift Certificates as Donations

A business owner wrote us, posing the following interesting question: "I followed the instructions in your book Running QuickBooks Premier Editions for setting up gift certificates, and everything posts perfectly. Now, in addition to selling gift certificates, I want to give gift certificates to local charitable groups, so they can use them for awards. The steps I use to record the sale of a gift certificate don't work, because no money is deposited to my bank account. In addition, I want the tax exemption for a charitable gift to show up on my corporate financial reports. Do I need to set up special items for this situation?"

You don't need an item, because there's no sale. In fact, there's no exchange of money, so there's no need to open a sales transaction window. When you give the certificate to the charitable organization, make the following journal entry:

Credit the liability account you set up for gift certificates, and debit the contributions expense account.

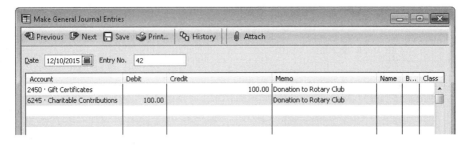

When the holder of the certificate shops for goods and uses the certificate for payment, follow the same steps you use when a customer uses a gift certificate that was purchased:

1. Enter the item(s) the customer buys (credit to the income account connected to the item).

2. Enter the item you created for gift certificates that are being cashed in, and use a minus sign for the amount (debit to the gift certificate liability account). Don't use

the item you created for the sale of a gift certificate, which is a Payment item, not a Sales item.

3. If the purchases are less than the amount of the certificate, issue a new certificate for the balance (using the steps for selling a gift certificate). If the purchase total is more than the amount of the certificate, the cash you collect appears in the Make Deposits window.

Donation as a Customer Credit

An accountant has a nonprofit customer with a balance due of $500.00. The customer is having its annual fundraising affair, and tickets are $100.00. The accountant agreed to buy a ticket and take the amount off the balance due. However, the accountant wants to show the $100.00 as a charitable donation. He wants to know if there's an easy way to do this.

There's a way to do this, but whether it's easy depends on your definition of that word. What makes the process a bit more convoluted is the need to have an Item available in order to fill out a sales or customer credit transaction.

You can't just post the credit to a Donation expense account, you have to create an item for Donations, and link it to your Donation expense account (an Other Charge or Service Item works best). When you create the Credit Memo, select the Donation item and enter the appropriate amount. When QuickBooks warns you that the item is connected to an expense account, click **OK** to continue.

Warning

⚠ This item is associated with an expense account.
Do you want to continue?

☐ Do not display this message in the future

[OK]   [Cancel]

Apply the credit to an invoice (or to multiple invoices if no single invoice is as large as the credit). If you want to show the credit as a specific line item in the customer's statement, don't apply the credit to an invoice when you create it — retain the credit and apply it against the next customer payment.

Tracking Inventory Given to a Charity

A reader wrote to ask how account for inventory that was donated to a charitable organization. He created a zero-based invoice for the customer/charity but that didn't track the amount he donated to charity.

The best way to accomplish this is to use the Adjust Inventory transaction window. Instead of using your normal Inventory Adjustment account in the Adjustment Account field, use the Charitable Donations expense account.

CHAPTER 7: CHART OF ACCOUNTS TIPS

The chart of accounts is the list of account names you use to keep your accounting records. Each name in the list represents a category for the type of transactions that are collected for that name. For example, there are accounts for assets (bank account, equipment), liabilities (loans payable, sales tax payable), income (sales), and expenses (payroll, rent, etc.).

Although the chart of accounts is merely a list of names (and numbers, if you elect to use a numbered chart of accounts), it is the foundation of your ledger (usually called the General Ledger). All of your individual transaction postings make up the totals in your general ledger.

Linking a transaction to an account is called posting. For instance, when you deposit money from the sale of goods or services into your bank, you post the transaction amount to the bank that's in your chart of accounts (that's the debit side of the transaction), and the income category in your chart of accounts (that's the credit side). When you send a check to the landlord, you post the transaction to the expense named Rent (the debit side) in your chart of accounts, and remove the money from the bank (the credit side).

–Excerpt from **Accounting Savvy for Business Owners**
by Phillip B. Goodman CPA (available at www.cpa911.com)

See All Account Balances in the Chart of Accounts Window

By default, the QuickBooks Chart of Accounts (COA) window displays the balances only for Assets, Liabilities, and Equity (Balance Sheet accounts). To see the balance of an Income or Expense account you must open the account. You can change this view, but you need to understand the data you see.

By default, the balances for Balance Sheet accounts in QuickBooks are displayed in a column named Balance Total. To show the balances of all accounts, follow these steps:

1. Right-click anywhere in the COA window and choose **Customize Columns**.to display the Customize Columns dialog box.

2. In the left pane select **Balance** and click **Add** to add the Balance Column to the COA window.

3. Click **OK** to return to the Chart of Accounts Window.

Now you have two balance columns: Balance (which displays the current balance for every account) and Balance Total (which displays the current balance for every Balance Sheet account).

Name	Type ▲	Balance Total	Attach	Balance
◆270000 · Bank Loan #445	Long Term Liability	5,054.20		0.00
◆270010 · Bank Loan 445 Receipts	Long Term Liability	5,154.20		-5,154.20
◆270020 · Bank Loan 445 Credits	Long Term Liability	-100.00		100.00
◆3000 · Opening Bal Equity	Equity	0.00		0.00
◆313000 · Owner's Capital	Equity	-2,200.00		0.00
◆315000 · Draws	Equity	-2,800.00		2,800.00
◆315100 · Personal payment of bus exp	Equity	600.00		-600.00
◆390000 · Retained Earnings	Equity			-250.00
◆391000 · Unrestricted net assets	Equity	0.00		0.00
◆400000 · Income	Income			-131,608.40
◆4000 · Consulting	Income			-1,471.55
◆401000 · Product Sales	Income			-48,444.20
◆402000 · Other Regular Income	Income			-42,049.90
◆4025 · Finance Charges Collected	Income			-657.84
◆404000 · Reimbursed Expenses	Income			-383.00
◆405000 · Discounts Taken	Income			-29.67
◆406000 · Overpayments	Income			-0.64
◆499999 · Write-offs	Income			4,422.56
◆500000 · Cost of Goods Sold	Cost of Goods Sold			15,494.51
◆500100 · Inventory Adjustments	Cost of Goods Sold			1,004.00
◆500200 · Damaged Inventory	Cost of Goods Sold			0.00
◆409000 · Discounts Given	Expense			-2.93
◆600000 · Salaries and Wages	Expense			-1,000.00
◆600100 · Salaries-Officers	Expense			1,000.00

There are some other differences between the Balance column and the Balance Total column:

In the Balance column (whichs shows the current balance for every account in QuickBooks), if you have subaccounts the parent account balance should be zero. (If a parent account balance isn't zero, you've posted transactions to the parent account, which you should never do.)

The Balance Total column (which displays balances for QuickBooks Balance Sheet accounts) shows the total of the parent account for any Balance Sheet account that has subaccounts (the total should equal the sum of the subaccount balances).

Additionally, in the Balance column the amounts displayed reflect the way debits and credits are posted in QuickBooks. Because there aren't two columns within this column (one for debits and a separate one for credits), you see the following:

- Income accounts normally display a negative number (these are credit-side accounts.)
- Expense accounts normally display a positive number (these are debit-side accounts.)

Advantage of Account Numbers

A reader wrote to complain that his accountant wanted him to use account numbers, and he doesn't understand why this is an advantage. He likes the idea that he can start typing the letters for an account name when he's using a drop-down list, and QuickBooks will find the account quickly.

First of all, if you're using account numbers, typing the account name to move quickly to the account still works.

The big advantage of account numbers is that you can arrange your chart of accounts more efficiently. For example, it's difficult to keep similar expenses together without numbers, because without numbers, QuickBooks sorts the chart of accounts alphabetically. This is especially handy if you export reports to Excel and want to create subtotals; something accountants do frequently to subtotal groups of contiguous accounts to match the totals required on tax returns.

Re-ordering the Account List on Reports

A reader wrote to ask how to fix a problem he's having when he prints his P & L Statement and Balance Sheet. He uses account numbers and the accounts aren't being displayed in numerical order. The accounts are in order when he views the list in the Chart of Accounts List window, but not on his reports.

We've seen this occur many times, even when account numbers aren't used — reports print with accounts of the same type (e.g. expenses) out of alphabetical order. We don't know why it occurs, and we have a fix, and we don't know why this fix works, it just does.

1. Press **Ctrl-A** to open the Chart of Accounts.
2. Click the **Account** button at the bottom of the window.
3. From the menu that appears, select the command **Re-sort List**.

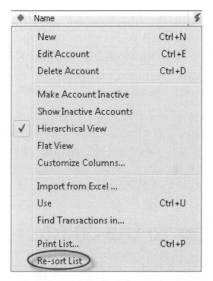

4. When QuickBooks asks if you're sure you want to return the list to its original order, click **OK**.

Removing Account Numbers in Reports

If you need to print financial statements without displaying account numbers, the solution is simple.

1. Select **Edit | Preferences** from the menu bar to open the Preferences dialog box.

2. Click the **Accounting** icon in the left pane and the **Company Preferences** tab in the right pane.

3. Deselect the **Use Account Numbers** option (remove the checkmark).

4. print the reports. The accounts will display alphabetically by account type.

5. After you print the reports, reopen the Preferences dialog and re-enable account numbers (add a checkmark to the Use Account Numbers option).

This is a useful trick when you're printing financial information for somebody who isn't familiar with your chart of accounts. When accounts appear alphabetically, it's easier for the reader, perhaps a banker, to find specific account names. (Of course, this assumes the accounts are named in a logical fashion, clearly indicating each account's use.)

Prevent Changes to the Chart of Accounts

A reader wrote to say that he wants to stop users from adding or changing accounts without preventing them from entering and editing transactions.

Edit the user permissions so that the option labeled No Access is selected for Sensitive Accounting Activities.

Bank Balance is Different in Balance Sheet

A reader wrote with the following problem: "When I ran this month's balance sheet, the bank balance differed from the amount displayed in the Chart of Accounts window. I ran the report on the last day of the month, so it's not a date difference. I ran the Verify feature and the file is fine. What could cause this problem?"

When this occurs, it almost always means that the bank balance displayed in the COA window includes transactions dated beyond the current date. Open the bank register and look for post-dated transactions (QuickBooks displays a blue line in the register above transactions dated in the future).

The bank balance above the blue line should match your balance sheet amount. One common cause is post-dated paychecks, because many bookkeepers prepare payroll at the end of the payroll period and the paycheck date is later than the last date of the payroll period.

Changing Account Numbers

Readers frequently write to ask us how to increase the number of digits in their account numbers. Usually, they want more digits so they can fine-tune their chart of accounts and they're running out of numbers. Many of these readers have figured out that the way to increase the number of digits is to open each account and type in a new number (you can use up to seven digits, and many readers have company files that have been in use since early versions of QuickBooks, when the default number of digits was four).

Changing account numbers one at a time is onerous, time consuming, and exceedingly annoying. Here's a better way.

1. Choose **File | Utilities | Export | Lists To IIF Files** to display the Export dialog box.
2. Select **Chart of Accounts** as the list to be exported.

Export

Select the lists that you would like to export.

☑ Chart of Accounts	☐ Payment Terms List	OK
☐ Customer List	☐ Payment Method List	Cancel
☐ Vendor List	☐ Shipping Method List	Help
☐ Employee List	☐ Customer Message List	
☐ Other Names List	☐ Budgets	
☐ Customer Type List	☐ To Do Notes	
☐ Vendor Type List	☐ Sales Rep List	
☐ Class List	☐ Price Level List	
☐ Job Type List	☐ Sales Tax Code List	
☐ Item List		

3. Click **OK** to display another Export dialog (this one is really a Windows "Save" dialog.

4. Select a location to save the exported list to and give it an appropriate name (e.g. "Chart of Accounts List.iif").

5. Click **OK** to save the file.

6. Open Windows Explorer or My Computer and locate the saved file.

7. Open it in Excel and change the account numbers in the ACCNUM column.

You can use Excel's shortcut functions to automate this process.

For example, let's say your Insurance Expenses are currently numbered 6100 for Insurance (the parent account) and you have subaccounts numbered 6110-Automobile, 6120-Building, 6130-Liability, 6140-Workers Comp, and so on. You want to move to a six-digit account number. In Excel, change 6100 to 610000, and change 6110 to 610100. Select both cells and drag down to see that Excel will follow this pattern, numbering the next account 610200, and continuing the pattern.

Even if you're going to enter the new account numbers manually, it's faster in Excel than in QuickBooks, where you have to select each account, press Ctrl-E to edit the account, enter the new number, and click OK.

Save the Excel file as an IIF file (which is really a delimited text file) and import it back into your company file (Files | Utilities | Import | IIF Files).

CHAPTER 8:

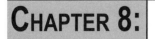

ESCROW ACCOUNTS TIPS

Money that is deposited into an escrow account comes from a third party for the benefit of a client. This is not income. You deposit the money by posting the transaction to the liability account you set up to track escrow funds, as seen in Table 6-8. You must also include the transaction in the client's record (software does this automatically, because you receive the money using the client as the customer).

ACCOUNT	DEBIT	CREDIT
1050 - Escrow Bank Account	10000.00	
2600 - Funds Held in Trust		10000.00

Table 6-8: Escrow funds are always posted to the liability account that tracks escrow.

–Excerpt from **Accounting Savvy for Business Owners**
by Phillip B. Goodman CPA (available at www.cpa911.com)

Moving Funds Between Escrow Liability Accounts

A reader wrote to say she has several liability accounts for tracking funds held in escrow bank accounts, and she had to move funds between two escrow liability accounts. She used the Transfer Funds transaction window to accomplish her task, but the amounts posted backwards. The account that was supposed to receive the money had the amount reduced, and vice-versa.

The Transfer Funds feature in QuickBooks is designed for asset accounts, where positive numbers (debits) increase amounts, and negative numbers (credits) decrease accounts.

Because liability accounts are tracked as negative numbers in QuickBooks, the Transfer Funds feature works backwards for these accounts. The solution is to enter the transaction backwards, selecting the receiving account as the "From" account, and the contributing account as the "To" account.

It might be a better idea to use a journal entry instead of the Transfer Funds transaction window. However, if you use a JE, remember that in order to increase a liability account you must credit the amount (and debit the account you're decreasing).

Setting Up Mortgage Accounts

This is a question that comes up regularly… "how do I set up a mortgage in QuickBooks that includes taxes and insurance that are held in escrow?"

It's a simple matter of setting up the necessary accounts and making the correct monthly postings.

1. Press **CTRL-A** to open the Chart of Accounts
2. Press **CTRL-N** to display the Add New Account dialog.
3. Choose **Other Account Types** and select **Long Term Liability** from the drop down list.

4. Click **Continue** and enter the account name (something like Mortgage Payment) and number. If you have more than one mortgage outstanding you might want to enter a description to ensure you don't get them confused.

5. Click **Save & New** and repeat the process to create an expense account called Interest Expense, and an other current asset account called Escrow.

6. When you make your payment, press CTRL-W to open the Write Checks window.

7. Select the appropriate bank account from the Bank Account drop down list.

8. Enter the name of the mortgage holder as the payee.

9. Enter the date and the amount of the payment.

10. Move to the Expenses tab and select the Mortgage Payment account from the Account drop down list.

11. Tab to the Amount field and enter the part of the payment that is going toward the mortgage principal. You should have an amortization schedule from the lending institution, that gives you the breakdown of each payment.

12. Move to the next line and select the Interest Expense account and enter the amount of the interest portion. As you enter each amount, QuickBooks recalculates the remaining balance and moves it to the next line.

13. On the third line choose the Escrow account, which should have the proper amount entered already.

```
Write Checks - Operating Account

Previous   Next   Save   Print ▼   Find   Attach

Bank Account  100000 · Operating Account  ▼      Ending Balance   127,143.04

                                          No.    1567
                                          Date   12/01/2015
Pay to the Order of  MyBank                $   1,589.46

One thousand five hundred eighty-nine and 46/100************************ Dollars

         MyBank
Address

Memo     Acct# 123456789                                          Order Checks

Expenses   $1,589.46   Items        $0.00   □ Online Payment   □ To be printed

Account              Amount    Memo              Customer:...  Billa...  Class
27100 · Mortgage Payment  1,000.00  Principal
6200 · Interest Expense    400.00  Interest
151500 · Escrow            189.46  Taxes & Insurance

Clear Splits   Recalculate          Save & Close   Save & New   Clear
```

Click **Save & Close**, print the check and mail it, and you're done.

CHAPTER 9:

FIXED ASSET TIPS & TRICKS

A fixed asset is something that a business owns and uses to run the business and produce income. Fixed assets are not expected to be consumed or sold in less than a year, and they therefore are categorized as Long Term Assets. Fixed assets are tangible: you can see them, touch them, and point them out. The common categories of fixed assets are:

- *Equipment (office and plant equipment)*
- *Furniture & Fixtures*
- *Vehicles*
- *Buildings*
- *Leasehold Improvements (for improvements you make to real estate you're renting)*

–Excerpt from **Accounting Savvy for Business Owners**
by Phillip B. Goodman CPA (available at www.cpa911.com)

Depreciating Fixed Assets

After your accountant calculates the depreciation for assets, you must do a journal entry to decrement the amount of the asset by the amount of depreciation. Many people make the following entry:

ACCOUNT	DEBIT	CREDIT
Equipment		Amt of Depreciation
Depreciation Expense	Amt of Depreciation	

As a result, the Balance Sheet shows the current value of the asset (after depreciation). That's mathematically correct. However, you don't have any history unless you took the time and trouble to keep records outside of your accounting software (which is silly because you purchased accounting software to avoid all that manual work).

Here's a better way: Use subaccounts. Create the primary account as Automobiles. Then create two subaccounts:

- Automobile (for the asset)
- Accum Depr-Auto (for the depreciation)

You never post anything to the parent account; it's just there to hold the subaccounts. Post the original value of the automobile in the Automobile subaccount, then use the Accum Depr- Automobile account for your year-end journal entry (against the Depreciation Expense).

Now your balance sheet shows the original worth of the asset as well as the depreciation that's been applied over the years. The math is right, it nets out to the current worth. When you print your balance sheet it shows the following:

Account	Debit	Credit
Automobiles		
Automobile(Jaguar)	90,000	
Accum Depr(Jaguar)		40,000
Total for Automobiles	50,000	

Tracking Maintenance Costs for Fixed Assets

A reader wrote to ask the best way to track the cost of maintaining his vehicle assets. He said he created a separate asset listing for each vehicle (using subaccounts under the Fixed Assets- Vehicles account). He wanted to know if he could create a third level account for maintenance expenses, creating another subaccount under each vehicle's subaccount.

Generally, maintenance expenses are real expenses, and if you post them to an asset account they won't reduce your income on your Profit & Loss Statement. To track the expense for each vehicle, create an expense account named Vehicle Expenses and then create a subaccount for each vehicle.

After we published that article, a reader wrote with another solution, one that works especially well if you have more than a couple of vehicles. Here's her solution:

Set up a Customer for the business vehicles and add each vehicle as a job. Make sure that the "jobs" are linked to every vendor bill or direct disbursement check for vehicle maintenance. This makes the P & L report less complicated. Bravo! Our subscribers come up with fantastic suggestions.

CHAPTER 10:

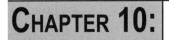

JOURNAL ENTRY TIPS

Every transaction you enter results in a journal entry. For example, if you created a check to pay the rent, the journal for the transaction resembles the journal in Table 2-1.

ACCOUNT	DEBIT	CREDIT
1000 - Bank Account		800.00
6000 - Rent	800.00	

Table 2-1: The journal tracks each transaction you create.

If you use accounting software, the journal is created automatically. In fact, in addition to tracking the accounts involved in each transaction, accounting software can provide reports about transactions for other entities in your bookkeeping records, such as the customer, vendor, inventory item, and so on.

TIP: Many accounting software applications let you view the journal from the original transaction's window. For example, in QuickBooks you can open a transaction and press **Ctrl-Y** to see the journal.

Journals can track additional information you record in addition to the accounts and amounts, such as the reference number for the source document (invoice number, check number) and the vendor or customer involved in the transaction.

–Excerpt from **Accounting Savvy for Business Owners**
by Phillip B. Goodman CPA (available at www.cpa911.com)

Journal Entries for Payables and Receivables

> ***Publisher's Note***: *Although changes in QuickBooks 2011 and QuickBooks 2012 have eliminated part of the problem presented in this reader's question, we've decided to include it for users of older versions.*

We're covering this topic again because it keeps coming up. This week's large number of messages asking for help is similar to the hundreds of messages we receive every week - here's one of the messages, and its text is typical:

"I needed to write off an amount from a vendor, so our accountant created a Journal Entry that debited A/P and credited the original expense. In my Trial Balance and my Balance Sheet, the A/P account now has a zero balance. However the original bill shows up on the aging report as unpaid. I went on to one of the QuickBooks forums and was told to edit the Journal Entry to include the vendor's name Now, my aging report, and my vendor report for that vendor, show two open transactions, the original unpaid bill balance, and the amount from the Journal Entry. My accountant says that all the entries were to the proper accounts and he doesn't know why my aging report for the vendor shows these two transactions. Meanwhile, when I create vendor reports for my boss, he's demanding to know why he sees open transactions, and he's really upset that the original bill is still showing up with a balance in the Unpaid Bills report."

> ***Publisher's Note:*** *Current versions of QuickBooks will no longer allow you to create a journal entry using an A/R or A/P account without entering a customer or vendor name. Also, while both transactions appear on the Unpaid Bills report, the report now shows a balance of zero.*

(You can substitute customer for vendor and A/R for A/P in the message, because this occurs just as often for customer transactions.)

The solution is to open the Pay Bills window and select the open bill, and then apply the credit that was created by the JE to that bill.

LISTEN UP! A Journal Entry is NOT a proper transaction type for customer/vendor credits (nor for many other transaction types). Instead, create a Credit transaction and apply it to the open balance of the original transaction.

Accountants (and, to be fair, some users) use JEs too often because it's a quick and easy way to complete a task. They either don't know or don't care that this action doesn't really adjust vendor/customer records; it just changes the bottom line. Users are left with open bills in the Pay Bills window, or customer invoices in the Receive Payments window. Reports show individual transactions with balances. QuickBooks has no way to connect a credit balance from a JE with an open balance from a transaction, so the transaction list on a vendor or customer report grows long (although it mathematically balances to zero).

Many users have asked their accountants to stop using JEs except for real adjustments (such as depreciation). If your accountant doesn't know how to create a credit in QuickBooks and apply it to an open transaction, do it yourself, don't let anyone "solve" your write-off problem with a Journal Entry; that just creates extra work.

Reversing Journal Entries

A reader wrote to ask about the value of auto-reversing journal entries, including the question "why not just delete the original journal entry to reverse it?"

A reversing JE is one in which on a certain date the financial reports include the amounts posted by the JE, and on a later date, the reports don't include that amount. Since QuickBooks' reports are date sensitive, this is a very useful feature.

Usually, the JE is dated the last day of a period (year, quarter, etc.) and the reversal entry is dated the next day. Premier Accountants Edition has reversing JEs built in, but you can create an auto-reversing JE in any edition of QuickBooks by making a JE as of a certain date, and then creating a separate JE with the next day's date that reverses the postings.

Finding Previous Journal Entries

A reader wrote to ask, "When I need to look at a journal entry I made a while ago, I have to click the Previous button through every journal entry until I come to the one I want. Is there an easier way to do this?"

The answer is yes. Run a report of journal entries.

1. Choose **Reports | Accountant & Taxes | Journal**.
2. Click **Customize Report** (Modify Report in pre-QuickBooks 2012 versions) and move to the Filters tab.
3. In the Choose Filter list, select **Transaction Type**.
4. Then, from the Transaction Type drop down list, select **Journal**.

5. Memorize the report so you don't have to go through these steps again.

In QuickBooks Premier Accountant Edition, there's a Reports icon on the Make General Journal Entries transaction window - just select the report you need.

Journal Entries with No Amounts on the First Line

In our last newsletter, we explained how to use a JE to pay bills using a Line of Credit account. In our explanation, we said to make sure the first line of the JE only contains text in the Memo section, and to begin entering accounts and amounts on the second line.

We heard from several readers that if you don't have financial data in the first line of a JE, you can't open the transaction when you drill down to its listing in reports. That's true, and if that's important, you can start entering financial data in the first line of the JE.

HOWEVER, you must understand the way QuickBooks reports information contained in JEs. The concepts of Source Account and Target Account are terribly important for getting accurate reports. You can learn more about the way QuickBooks tracks Source and Target in the following article titled "The Mystery of Sources and Targets."

The Mystery of Sources and Targets

All transactions in QuickBooks have a source and a target, and if you don't get them right, you end up with unexpected results.

The source is the account where the transaction originates, and the target is the account where it is completed. When you write a check to a vendor, the bank account is the source (it's where the money starts) and the expense account is the target (it's where the money ends up).

If you attach additional information to the check, it travels with its source or target counterpart. For example, assigning a customer to the line that contains an expense account (for job costing) links the customer information and the amount to the target (because a line item is part of the target).

The following is an excerpt from **Running QuickBooks 2012 Premier Editions** *by Kathy Ivens and Tom Barich (available at www.cpa911.com)*

JE Source and Target: Solving the Mystery

One common use of a JE is to allocate an expense across jobs to track job costs. It's easy, you debit the same expense account multiple times in order to select a customer or job for each applicable portion of the expense, and credit the original expense total so the general ledger totals aren't changed. You can do the same type of JE to allocate costs (usually overhead) across classes. Table 4-1 is a representation of a JE designed to track job costs.

Account	Debit	Credit	Memo	Name
Shipping		200.00	Allocation	
Shipping	100.00		Allocation	Cust:Job #1
Shipping	50.00		Allocation	Cust:Job #2
Shipping	50.00		Allocation	Cust:Job #3

Table 4-1: Allocate expenses to track the cost of jobs.

After performing this task, it's a common complaint that the job costing reports don't show the expenses that were allocated in the journal entry. If you run an Unbilled Costs By Job report, some or all of the data in your JEs doesn't appear. If you marked the amount as billable in the JE, the billable costs show up when you invoice the customer, they just don't show up in reports.

Often, when you create a JE that moves expenses from one customer to another, the wrong customer receives the cost posting.

What's going on? The answer is that all transactions in QuickBooks have a source and a target, and if you don't get them right, you end up with unexpected results.

The source is the account where the transaction originates, and the target is the account where it is completed. When you write a check to a vendor, the bank account is the source (it's where the money starts) and the expense account is the target (it's where the money ends up).

If you attach additional information to the check, it travels with its source or target counterpart. For example, assigning a customer to the line that contains an expense account (for job costing) links the customer information and the amount to the target (because a line item, in which this data exists, is part of the target).

For JEs that perform job costing allocations there are two important facts to remember:

- QuickBooks assigns job costing or other information when it's part of the target, and ignores it when it is part of the source.
- The first line of a JE is the source and all other lines are targets.

This means that if you're moving job costing information from one customer to another or from one job to another for the same customer, you will almost certainly end up with one or more incorrect postings.

Creating JEs With No Source Accounts

I've learned that to play it safe, the best way to create a JE that's connected to job costing is to make every line in the transaction part of the target. Remembering that only the first line is the source, the solution is to avoid using the first line for anything "real."

In the first line of a JE, enter only a memo. Starting with the second line, enter real information. Because everything is a target, everything posts appropriately, and you can create reports that show your activities.

If you've already encountered the source/target problem, you don't have to void and re-enter all the journal entries that had a source/target mix up. Just edit the journal entry to change the source line, as follows:

1. Open the JE transaction and click anywhere in the first line to select that line.
2. Press CTRL-INS (or CTRL-INSERT, depending on the label your keyboard uses) to insert a blank line above the current first line.
3. Enter text in the Memo field to create a source line.
4. Close the Make General Journal Entries transaction window.
5. QuickBooks displays a message that you've changed the transaction and asks if you want to save it.
6. Click **Yes**.

Everything posts correctly.... but you may have another problem. When you insert a line in a previous JE, QuickBooks loses track of the automatic numbering feature for JEs. In fact, the JE number may disappear from the JE window. Before you close the window, re-enter the JE number to kick-start automatic numbering again.

Solving Source-Target Mysteries in Reports

Here's another mystery that's solved if you understand the QuickBooks source/target paradigm. Unfortunately, solving the mystery doesn't always remove the problem. Here's a puzzle I was presented with. To guess how I solved it, you have to remember that the target, not the source, has dibs on reports about postings.

An accountant called me from a client site. He was grumpy. Here's the transcript of our conversation.

Him: I'm looking at a trial balance and my client has several expense accounts that have postings for consultants that get 1099s so I'm checking his 1099 payments. When I double-click one of those accounts, I get a QuickReport.

Me: Right, that's what's supposed to happen.

Him: The payees are wrong. I asked my client who Sam Smith is and why he's not listed as a 1099 vendor, and he tells me Sam Smith is a customer. I asked him why he was writing checks to Sam Smith, and he says he's not.

Me: Double-click the listing for the check to Sam Smith - you'll see the original check.

Him: OK, the check is made out to somebody else, why does the report say Sam Smith?

Me: Check the columns in the line item section. I'll bet he linked the expense to a customer named Sam Smith.

Him: That's right. So I have to keep double-clicking every single entry, all hundreds of them, to find out who the payee really is because this report is wrong?

Me: Nope, click **Customize Report** (Modify Report in pre-QuickBooks 2012 versions) and deselect the Name listing and select the Source Name listing.

Reports on disbursements should provide information on the source name by default, saving the use of the target name for job costing reports. I've passed my thoughts on this to Intuit, but I haven't received any response.

You need to be aware of the fact that when you create a report to get information about disbursements and expenses, you may end up with some very confusing data in the report. If an expense is linked to a customer (target data), that's the name that appears on the report. If no expenses are linked to customers or jobs, the payee (source data) appears. Most of the time, modifying the report to display Source Name instead of Name (which really means target name if a target name exists) cures the problem.

If you have some reason to know both the source and target names, select both from the Display list. For those transactions without a posting to a target name, both columns have the same data (the source name)—but it would be clearer if the target name column were blank.

CHAPTER 11: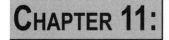

LINES OF CREDIT TIPS

A line of credit is like a loan that you can use if and when the need arises. The advantage of a line of credit over a loan is that interest is charged only on the amount of the line of credit that you have drawn from the total amount available. A line of credit is issued with a maximum amount, but you only need to track the amount you've drawn and is therefore outstanding.

There are a variety of plans that financial institutions use to award and track a line of credit, but for this discussion I'll assume your line of credit follows the common scenario:

- *When you need to draw on the line of credit, the financial institution transfers the amount you request into your bank account.*

- *The financial institution collects interest on the amount currently drawn. (Frequently the interest is automatically deducted from your bank account).*

- *There are no regularly scheduled payments for repaying principal.*

–Excerpt from **Accounting Savvy for Business Owners**
by Phillip B. Goodman CPA (available at www.cpa911.com)

Tracking a Line of Credit

We get a lot of questions from users about tracking a line of credit in QuickBooks. Actually, this isn't terribly complicated. You just have to remember a few rules:

- You must set up a liability account for the line of credit.

- You must have an expense account for interest paid (you don't have to create a specific account for the line of credit).

- Do not enter the total available line of credit in the liability account; instead, enter only what you take (pull down). Your liability is only the amount you use, not the amount the bank offers to provide.

When you draw money from the line of credit and put it into your bank account (either by direct transfer through the bank or by using a check from a checkbook provided for the line of credit) use one of the following actions:

- Use the Make Deposits window. Enter the amount you are depositing, and post it to the liability account for this line of credit.

- Create a journal entry, debiting the checking account and crediting the liability account.

If your line of credit came with its own checkbook, and you use a line of credit check to pay a vendor, use a journal entry to credit the liability account and debit the expense. Remember to enter the vendor's name in the journal entry to track the vendor.

You could also set up a bank account for the line of credit checks, use the Write Checks transaction window to pay the vendor, and post the amount to the liability account instead of an expense account.

When you make a payment on your line of credit, enter the transaction in the bank register for the account from which you're drawing the payment funds. Enter a check number if you write a check, or enter BT (Bank Transfer) if you instructed your bank to transfer the funds. Post the principal amount to the line of credit liability account, and post the interest amount to your Interest expense account.

After we published this article, a reader wrote to suggest that another way to track a line of credit is to set up the line as a credit card liability account. This lets you track the interest the bank is applying (instead of tracking interest only when you make an interest payment). Thanks to Ron, a newsletter subscriber, for that suggestion.

Using a Line of Credit to Pay Vendors

A reader wrote the following: "I have a line of credit (LOC) with my bank and they gave me checks to use when I want to draw on the LOC. I want to use those checks to pay some of my vendors. My accountant said I have to enter each draw from the LOC into the liability account she set up to track the LOC. But the LOC doesn't appear in the list of banks in the Payment Account box at the bottom of the window when I use the Pay Bills window. How do I do this?"

An easy way to accomplish this is with a journal entry.

1. In the first line of the JE transaction window, enter the check number in the Memo field (don't enter any accounts or amounts).

2. In the second line, debit Accounts Payable for the amount of the check, enter the check number again, and be sure to select the Vendor in the Name column. (You're actually creating a vendor credit.)

3. In the third line, credit the LOC liability account for the amount of the check, and enter the check number again.

4. Open the Pay Bills window, select the appropriate vendor bill, and apply the credit. Now you can mail the check to the vendor.

(We recommend entering the check number in every line of the JE because it's the way to make sure you can find that data with any report you create if you have to discuss the payment with your vendor or with the bank.)

Another way to pay bills directly from your LOC account is to set up the account as a credit card account instead of a liability. When you select Credit Card in the Method of Payment field (at the bottom of the Pay Bills window), your credit card accounts appear in the drop-down list that appears in the Payment Account field.

CHAPTER 12: TIPS FOR NONPROFITS

Nonprofit accounting is more complicated than the accounting required for most small businesses. Because QuickBooks needs workarounds to function properly for nonprofits, a rather comprehensive understanding of the way QuickBooks works is required.

Almost half of the small nonprofits who ask me for help have turned their accounting chores over to a user with a minimal understanding of QuickBooks, almost no understanding of basic bookkeeping conventions, and no knowledge of accounting rules.

Many of these nonprofits use volunteers to keep their books, and the problems that accrue provide a living testament to the adage, "You get what you pay for." Accounting bills are high, the cost of the required outside audit for nonprofits that file Form 990 is enormous, and detailed information desired by board members and funding agencies is impossible to get (requiring the additional expense of even more accounting services).

A QuickBooks expert who understands how to set up and use classes effectively is the minimal requirement for your bookkeeper, and whatever you have to pay that person is much less than you'll have to pay accountants to examine every single transaction in order to provide the information you need.

It is always a conflict of interest for the Treasurer of the Board of Directors to be the bookkeeper. In many states it's not illegal for one person to do both jobs, but it is an inherent conflict of interest. The Treasurer is an "oversight" role, representing the board's interests by examining the work performed by the bookkeeper.

–Excerpt from **Running QuickBooks in Nonprofits: 2nd Edition** by Kathy Ivens (available at www.cpa911.com)

How to Use a QuickBoks Discount Item to Apply Nonprofit Scholarships

A nonprofit wanted to know how to show that they're providing scholarships to members who can't afford to pay fees for some activities. They need to track both the fee income and the scholarship expense in QuickBooks.

Begin by creating the expense account:

1. Press **CTRL-A** to open the Chart of Accounts window.
2. Press **CTRL-N** to display the Add New Account dialog.
3. Select **Expense** and click **Continue**.
4. Enter an account number in the Number field.
5. Enter **Scholarships** in the Account Name field.
6. Enter a description if it will help identify the account.
7. Click **Save & Close** to create the new expense account.

Next, you need a discount item:

1. Choose **Lists | Item List** from the menu bar to open the Item List window.
2. Press **CTRL-N** to open a New Item dialog box.
3. From the Type drop down list, select **Discount**.
4. Enter **Scholarships** in the Item Name/Number field.
5. Enter a description if you like.
6. Only enter a number in the Amount field if the scholarship is always (or almost always) for the same amount.
7. From the Account drop down list choose the Scholarships expense account you created earlier.
8. Click **OK** to save the new item.

Now create the sales transaction by entering the item for the fee and then enter the scholarship discount item. If the item doesn't have a pre-set amount, enter the amount you're awarding; QuickBooks automatically enters a minus sign because the item is of the type Discount.

Note: *Only QuickBooks Premier Nonprofit Edition provides "Donation" forms. However, you can create your own (as we did here) by customizing the standard sales receipt form that comes with all versions of QuickBooks. Detailed instructions are provided in* **Running QuickBooks in Nonprofits: 2nd Edition** *by Kathy Ivens (available at www.cpa911.com)*

Divide an Item Among Multiple Categories

The treasurer of a nonprofit organization asked how to manage invoices for quarterly dues when the dues are actually applied to several categories.

Create an item for each category and link each item to the appropriate income account. For example, you may have items for dues, capital improvements, tithes, etc.

If all the categories are linked to the same class (e.g. Unrestricted Funds), it's easiest to create a group of these items and use the group item on the invoice.

If each item is linked to a different class, you have enter each item as an individual line item on the invoice, linking each to the appropriate class.

Transferring a QuickBooks License

We're often asked whether a copy of QuickBooks can be given or sold to another user. Many of the readers who pose this question want to give last year's version to a nonprofit organization after they've upgraded to the new version. If they give the original CD to someone else, the new owner can't register the software; the license agreement you agree to when you install QuickBooks clearly says that the license cannot be transferred.

However, you can transfer a license by filling out a form on the following web page:

http://support.quickbooks.intuit.com/Support/transfer/transfer.aspx

Intuit charges $25.00 as a "processing fee" for this service.

Year-end Donor Reports for Nonprofits

Nonprofits are required to provide written acknowledgment of yearly contributions of $250.00 or more. The acknowledgement must contain the IRS-approved text about whether the organization provided any goods or services in exchange for the donation. It's a good idea to send a year-end letter to all donors, including those who contributed less than $250.00 during the calendar year, because the letter provides an opportunity to thank the donors and to appeal for further donations.

QuickBooks cannot produce this letter. You can either run a donor report and prepare the letters manually, or you can buy add-on software to produce the letters automatically.

We recommend the add-on software created by Beyond The Ledgers (www.beyondtheledgers.com). You can go directly to the information about the donor acknowledgment letter add-on by copying the following URL to your browser's Address Bar: http://www.beyondtheledgers.com/ index_files/DetailsV3.htm

(Full Disclosure Legal Stuff: CPA911 Publishing has an interest in this add-on, which we helped design.)

Assign Multiple Classes to a Paycheck

Several readers have asked, "How can I assign multiple classes to a single paycheck? The paycheck window has a single class designation, but we need to break down earnings by class."

This is especially important for nonprofit organizations, where an employee's time is almost always divided among several programs. To accomplish this, you must change the configuration of the paycheck window so that you can enter individual earnings amounts linked to a class.

1. Choose **Edit | Preferences** to open the Preferences dialog.
2. Select the **Payroll & Employees** icon in the left pane.
3. In the Company Preferences tab, check the **Job Costing And Class Tracking For Paycheck Expenses** option.
4. Then choose the option, Assign One Class Per **Earnings Item**.

An Invoice is Always a Receivable

A volunteer bookkeeper at a church wrote to ask for help. To request donations, the minister sends invoices to church members with a "suggested" amount. Most of the time, the suggested amount is not what's received, and often no donation arrives at all. The bookkeeper wants to know how to keep these transactions out of Accounts Receivable, or wants a method to reverse the receivable.

An invoice is a receivable, that's an accounting rule you can't overcome. The best way to ask for donations, including a suggested amount, is to send a letter, not an accounting transaction.

PART II

CUSTOMERS, VENDORS, & EMPLOYEES

CHAPTER 13: 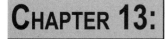 COMMISSIONS TIPS

I think the reason I'm asked so often about managing commissions for outside sales reps is the lack of an automatic commission calculator in QuickBooks. Some accounting applications let you enter the commission rate in the rep's record, and then automatically calculate the commission (and some software automatically creates the checks). QuickBooks doesn't, which makes the issue of sales reps and commissions seem more complicated than it is.

In order to track sales for which outside reps receive commission, you must create sales reps, and enter the rep on every affected sales transaction. (Chapter 2 covers setting up sales reps).

To enter the reps when you're creating transactions, you have to add the Sales Rep field to all the sales transaction templates you use (Sales Orders, Invoices, Sales Receipts, etc.). Some of the industry specific Premier editions provide a sales order template with the rep field included, but if such a template isn't available, create customized templates that contain a Rep field.

When a sales rep is linked to a customer, the rep's initials are automatically placed in the Rep field when that customer is selected in a sales transaction template. However, even if the rep is linked to that customer, if you use a transaction template without a Rep field, the transaction is not linked back to the rep.

–Excerpt from **Running QuickBooks 2012 Premier Editions**
by Kathy Ivens and Tom Barich (available at www.cpa911.com)

Paying Commissions on Paid Invoices Only

A reader wrote to ask how to create monthly reports to pay commissions to 1099 sales reps, because her company only pays the commissions when invoices are paid by the customers.

1. Choose **Reports | Sales | Sales By Rep Detail**.
2. Select the appropriate date range (usually Last Month if you're paying commissions for the month just ended).
3. Click **Customize Report** (Modify Report in pre-2012 QuickBooks versions) and select **Cash** as the Report Basis.

4. Click **OK** to display the customized report.

The report displays all invoices that were paid in the date range, as well as all cash receipts linked to the Rep.

Incidentally, we've found it a "best practice" to make sure that the Rep field appears on the templates you use for Invoices and Sales Receipts, so that QuickBooks can link each transaction to the appropriate Rep (rather than relying on the Rep configured for the customer in the customer's record).

Sales Reps Deduct Commissions

A business owner wrote to say he has two reps who often collect payment from customers when they're delivering products. The reps want to deduct their commissions and remit the balance. The owner doesn't know how to handle this in QuickBooks.

It's actually quite easy to manage this scenario. First you have to understand the basic rules:

- The customer's sale or invoice payment you post in QuickBooks must be the total paid by the customer.
- The reps must have their commissions tracked (especially if they're employees or 1099 recipients).

When you receive the revenue, enter the gross amount (which is not the amount of the net proceeds) in the sales transaction window (either Sales Receipt for a cash sale or Receive Payments if you issued an invoice).

Be sure you deposit the money to Undeposited Funds, not to a bank account. Then take the following steps:

1. From the menu bar, select **Banking | Make Deposits** to open the Payments to Deposit window.

2. Select this payment for deposit, and click **OK**. This opens the Make Deposits window.

3. Move to the row below the deposit and select the Rep's name from the Received From drop down list.

4. In the From Account drop down list, select the account you use for posting commissions (this account is linked to 1099 payments if the Rep gets a 1099).

5. Optionally, enter a comment in the Memo column (e.g. Commission on Inv1234).

6. Skip the Chk No. column.

7. Optionally, choose **Cash** in the Pmt. Meth. column.

8. Assign a class in the Class column (if you're tracking classes).

9. Enter the amount the Rep kept, as a negative amount in the Amount column.

10. Click **OK** to deposit the money into the bank.

The net amount is what you'll post to the bank account as a deposit. Your customer's record is accurate, and your rep's record is accurate.

Commissions on Items

A bookkeeper wrote to ask for help for a new client. She says she knows how to set up sales reps, assign them to customers, and add the Rep field to sales transactions, but her new client assigns reps to items, not customers. She wants to know how to track these reps so she can remit commissions. The solution is to add a custom field named REP to the Items List.

Then, customize a sales transaction template so that the REP column appears in the Screen version of the template (there's usually no reason to include the column in the printed version). You can customize sales reports to get the REP information you need.

Rep Commissions that Differ By Customer

A reader wrote to ask how to manage monthly rep commissions that differ by customer. The best way to do this is to create a custom field for each customer for the commission rate and also use the Rep field in every customer transaction.

Any report that lists the customer total sales, the custom field, and the rep name can be exported to Excel in order to calculate the commissions.

CHAPTER 14: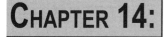

CREDIT CARDS TIPS

Not all bills fit neatly into one expense account. The bill you receive from your credit card company is a good example, because the line items on the bill probably cover multiple types of expenses. When you have multiple expense account postings for a single bill, the individual lines and their linked accounts are called the splits.

NOTE: *It's best to use one credit card for business and another credit card for personal use. This makes your accounting tasks easier. However, many proprietors don't follow this advice and I present these examples as a way to deal with reality.*

–Excerpt from **Accounting Savvy for Business Owners**
by Phillip B. Goodman CPA (available at www.cpa911.com)

Posting a Refund from a Credit Card Purchase

A reader purchased something on a credit card, and when she returned it she was given a check instead of a credit on her credit card. She doesn't know how to enter the refund in QuickBooks because she can't figure out its relationship to her credit card tracking. She also said she doesn't want to enter the vendor into the system.

This is easy because a refund is unconnected to credit card activity and you don't have to enter a vendor name to create a transaction.

1. Select **Banking | Make Deposits** to open the Make Deposits window.

2. Select the appropriate bank account and enter today's date.

3. Skip the Received From field.

4. In the From Account drop down list, select the expense account you used when you purchased the article.

5. Enter the check number, and select **Check** as the payment method.

6. Enter the amount of the refund check.

7. Click **Save & Close.**

That's all there is to it.

Displaying Bank and Credit Card Accounts on the Home Page

We get mail from readers complaining that they cannot see the list of bank accounts on the Home Page. They would like to see the accounts list because it's so easy to open a bank register from that list.

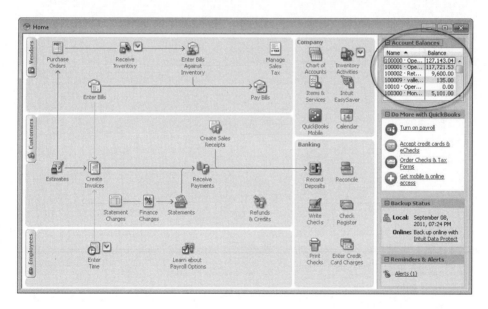

We also get mail from readers asking how they can prevent users from seeing the list of bank accounts on the Home Page (because the list shows the current balance and they don't want other users to know what the balance is). Credit card accounts are also included in this list.

The ability to see bank and credit card accounts, and their current balances, is dependent on user permissions. When you set up a user, or you edit a current user, you can enable/disable the ability to view this list.

1. Choose **Company | Set Up Users And Passwords | Set Up Users** to open the User List dialog box.

2. Select an existing user and click **Edit User** or click **Add User** to create a new user. Either choice opens the User And Password Access wizard. For this exercise we'll create a new user named Debbie.

3. Enter the user name and a password (twice for confirmation), and then click **Next** to view the access options screen.

4. Choose **Selected Areas Of QuickBooks** and click **Next** to begin setting access permissions for the user.

5. When you get to the wizard window named Sensitive Accounting Activities, choose either **No Access** or **Selected Access** (depending on the work the user does).

The account list only appears on the Home Page if Full Access is selected in this wizard window.

6. Continue through the wizard until you get to the summary screen.

7. Review the permissions and click **Finish** when you're satisfied.

This returns you to the User List dialog box. Now, click the **Close** button and you're done. When the new user, Debbie, logs into QuickBooks She will not be able view the account list on the Home Page.

Collecting Credit Card Sales for a Sister Company

A reader wrote, "We have a main company and a sister company, each with its own EIN number, so each has its own QuickBooks company file. Only the main company has a merchant account, and we don't want to open a second merchant account for the occasional credit card sale that the sister company has. If we use the main company to sell with a credit card, how do we track how much we owe to the sister company?"

Here's our solution:

1. Press **CTRL-A** to open the Chart of Accounts window
2. Press **CTRL-N** to display the Add New Account dialog.
3. Select **Other Account Types** and choose **Other Current Liability** from the drop down list.
4. Click **Continue** and fill in an account number and name the account Money Due to Sister Company, or something similar.

5. Next, you have to open the Item List and create items for those things you're selling for the sister company. Be sure to link them to Money Due to Sister Company account, instead of an income account.

6. At the end of the week, or month, or whenever you settle up, write a check for the amount of money in the Other Current Liability account, post the check to that account, and deposit it in the bank account of the sister company (don't forget that the sister company has to receive the income using a Sales Receipt).

If you run item reports for the items you sold using the appropriate date range, the quantity of each item shows, and the total sales should equal the amount of the check you wrote.

Reporting Posting Accounts for a Credit Card Payment

A reader wrote to ask how to show her boss the specific postings for a certain vendor bill when there are multiple accounts included in the bill. She explained that she pays credit card bills in full each month, so she doesn't track the individual transactions in a credit card account. The bill she enters contains multiple line items that post to multiple accounts, but there's no way to print the bill to show the postings to her boss.

Another reader wrote with the same question, except that this reader wrote direct checks instead of entering bills, and he needed to include the class to which each line item was linked in addition to the posting accounts.

Fortunately, you can view the individual posting in a Journal report:

1. Open the transaction in question.
2. Press **CTRL-Y** to view the Transaction Journal report for the transaction

We Do It All

Transaction Journal

All Transactions

Trans #	Type	Date	Num	Name	Memo	Account	Class	Debit	Credit
833	Check	12/31/2015	1564	Visa		100000 · Operating Account			1,774.40
				Visa		6170 · Equipment Rental		250.00	
				Visa		611500 · White Chevy Van		324.75	
				Visa		6550 · Office Supplies		187.44	
				Visa		6540 · Computer Supplies		632.15	
				Visa		611600 · Ford Taurus		190.25	
				Visa		6370 · Meals		189.81	
								1,774.40	1,774.40
TOTAL								**1,774.40**	**1,774.40**

CHAPTER 15:
CUSTOMER CREDITS TIPS

Customer credits are issued against the customer's current balance by applying the credit to an existing invoice, or by retaining the credit against future purchases (sometimes referred to as a floating credit).

When you issue a credit instead of a refund, the Accounts Receivable account is credited instead of the bank account.

All accounting software offers a customer credit transaction form, which produces the proper journal, and links the credit to the customer's record. If you're not using accounting software, a customer credit is a reverse invoice, so the journal posts the following transaction:

- *Accounts Receivable is credited (reduced).*
- *The appropriate income account is debited (reduced).*

–Excerpt from **Accounting Savvy for Business Owners**
by Phillip B. Goodman CPA (available at www.cpa911.com)

How to Swap Credits from One QuickBooks Job to Another

A reader wrote to ask our help. He has a customer with three jobs, all of which are completed. Two of the jobs have balances due, but the third job has a substantial outstanding credit for items that were returned after the job was finished. He wants to use the credit on the third job to pay off all of the first job and part of the second job. He wants to have a logical "trail" in QuickBooks to explain to the customer and to his accountant.

We found a way to accomplish this without changing the history of the original transactions that were applied to the three jobs in Quick-Books.

For this example, we used our customer named ContractorLarry, who had three jobs: Job01, Job02, Job03. Before the credit was issued, the following QuickBooks invoices and payments had been posted:

Job	Invoice	Payment	Balance
01	405.00	200.00	205.00
02	107.00	0.00	107.00
03	684.80	400.00	284.80

We then issued a credit to Job03 in the amount of $513.60. This created a credit balance for Job03 of $228.80. That credit amount is sufficient to pay off Job01 in full, and apply the remaining credit balance to the open balance for Job02.

We needed a place to "trade out" the credit from one job to another, so we created an account of the type Other Current Liability, which we named Customer Credits Exchange.

The first step was to move the credit amount into the Customer Credits Exchange account (so that we could use it for the other jobs), without removing the credit's history from Job03. We accomplished that with a journal entry that debited $228.80 to Accounts Receivable and credited the same amount to the Customer Credits Exchange account. Entering the job in the Name column created a receivable (invoice) against which we could wash the outstanding credit.

We opened the Receive Payments window and selected Job03, to display the ersatz invoice created by the debit side of the journal entry.

We left the Amount field at 0.00 and clicked the **Discounts & Credits** button to apply the existing credit to the new charge.

At this point, Job03 is at a zero balance, the job history has all the transactions that were applied, and the Customer Credits Exchange account has a credit balance of $228.80; we've moved the job credit to the balance sheet.

Next, we have to use $205.00 of the credit balance in the Customer Credits Exchange account to pay off Job01. In the Receive Payments transaction window, we selected Job01 to display the current balance due.

Leaving the Amount field at 0.00, we clicked **Discounts & Credits** and created a discount (not a credit) against the invoice in the amount of $205.00. We used the Customer Credits Exchange account as the Discount Account.

Job01 now had a zero balance and $23.80 remained in the Customer Credits Exchange account, which we applied against the balance for Job02 as a discount (same steps as applying the discount to Job01).

The Customer Credits Exchange account has been emptied, and the credit for Job03 has been applied to the other jobs.

Customer Credit for Damaged Product

A reader asked how to give a customer credit for a product that was faulty. He doesn't want the customer to return the product, because he doesn't want to pay for the shipping on a product he can't put back into the warehouse and sell. He entered a credit for the original item, but QuickBooks put the item back into inventory, which is not accurate.

There are two ways to resolve this:

1. After issuing the credit, do an inventory adjustment to remove the product.
2. Create an item named Damaged Returns and link it to an account named Returns (some accountants prefer the account name Returns and Allowances). Usually a return is a contra-income transaction so make the Returns account an income account. Use that item in the credit.

Writing Off Customer Credits

A reader wrote to say he was carrying credits for a few customers that are no longer in business, so he can't send them a check. He wants to know how to write off those credits. His bookkeeper wants to apply the credits to Other Income, and his accountant suggested he could apply the credits to his Bad Debt account to offset the current total in that account.

We have no suggestion about whether the credits should be posted to Other Income or Bad Debt (and we invite reader opinions about this), but here's the best way to accomplish this task:

1. Create an item for credit writeoffs (you can call it KillCredit, RemoveCredit, or any other name you come up with). Link the item to the appropriate account (Other Income or Bad Debt).

2. Create an invoice for each applicable customer in the amount of the credit balance.

3. Go to Receive Payments and apply the credit to the new invoice.

Moving an Applied Credit to a Different Invoice

A reader wrote to ask help with the following problem: "I applied a credit to a customer's invoice, and it should have been applied to the same customer, but a different invoice. I can't find a way to un-apply or move the credit amount."

You can change the invoice to which a credit was applied. This task requires several steps, but if you follow the instructions a step at a time, it's not as complicated as it seems.

1. Open the invoice to which you incorrectly applied the credit.

2. Click the **History** button at the top of the transaction window to display the list of all transactions linked to this invoice.

3. Click the listing for the credit you want to change, and click **Go To**, to open the original credit transaction.

4. Change the Customer:Job name to another customer. It doesn't matter which customer you choose because you're going to change it back (I've always had a customer named House to use for occasions like this and for other "tests" I want to run).

5. Click **OK** in any warning dialogs QuickBooks displays about the results of making this change.

6. Click **Save & Close**. QuickBooks warns you that you are breaking the connection.

7. Click **Yes** to confirm that you want to break the connection. Now you've destroyed the link between the credit and the invoice to which it was originally applied.

(QuickBooks returns you to the original invoice window, where the credit no longer appears in the History dialog.)

8. Open the credit transaction you just moved to another customer.

9. In the Create Credit Memos transaction window, change the customer name back to the original customer name.

10. Click **Save & Close** to close the transaction window.

When you save the transaction, QuickBooks offers the original choices for applying this credit. Choose to apply the credit to an existing invoice, and be sure to select the right invoice.

Make a Credit Memo a Pending Transaction

When you create a credit for a customer who is returning a product, technically the credit shouldn't be applied until you've received the returned product.

You can wait until the returned product arrives to issue the credit memo, but that means you have to remember that a credit is due. You can issue the credit, but that means you have to remember to keep an eye out for the returned product.

An often overlooked feature in the QuickBooks Credit Memo process can help.

1. After you create the credit, right-click a blank spot in the header or footer area of the Create Credit Memos/Refunds window.

2. From the shortcut menu that appears, select **Mark Credit Memo As Pending**.

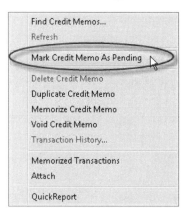

3. Once the Credit Memo is marked "Pending", click **Save & Close** to complete the procedure.

No amounts are posted to the General Ledger for a pending transaction, and inventory is not incremented.

When you receive the returned goods, follow the same proceducre:

1. Open the pending credit memo.
2. Right-click a blank spot in the header or footer area of the window.
3. Select **Mark Credit Memo As Final** from the shortcut menu that appears.

4. Click **Save & Close** to close the transaction window.
5. QuickBooks asks if you want to save your changes. Click **Yes**. The Available Credit dialog box opens, asking how to handle the credit.

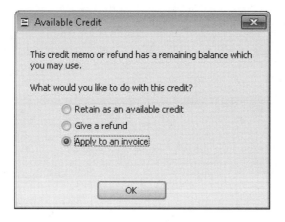

6. Make the appropriate selection and click **OK**.

> *TIP*: *To see all your pending transactions, choose **Reports
> | Sales | Pending Sales** from the QuickBooks menu bar.
> The report window displays both pending sales and pending
> credits. (Pending sales are a way to track backorders if
> you're not using a Premier or Enterprise edition of
> QuickBooks.)*

Reporting on Open Credits

If you want to see a report on open credits, start by selecting the Open
Invoices report, which displays all open invoices and open credits.

1. Select **Reports | Customers & Receivables | Open
   Invoices** from the menu bar.
2. Click the **Customeze Report** button (Modify Report in
   older versions) to display the Modify Report dialog box.
3. Click the **Filters** tab to access the report filtering
   options.
4. From the Filter list choose **Transaction Type**.
5. Now, select **Credit Memo** from the Transaction Type
   drop down list.

6. Click **OK** to save the changes.
7. Press **Ctrl-M** and memorize the report for future use.

You can also produce an open credits report for a specific customer or job. In addition to the previous customization steps, on the Filters tab choose **Name** from the Filter list. Then select the customer or job from the Name drop-down list.

Tracking Credits Applied to Invoices

A reader wrote to ask how to track credits that were applied to an invoice. He said he couldn't find a sales report that links credits to the invoices against which the credits were applied.

It's true that sales reports don't link credits to invoices (or payments to invoices for that matter). However, if you open an invoice you can click the History button at the top of the transaction window to display the applied credits and payments.

If you open a credit memo transaction, the History button tells you the invoice against which that credit was applied.

Mystery Credit Balances

Several times each week we receive a query that reads something like this: "Many of my customers have credit balances, and I've never used the Credit Memo function. What is going on?" When we write back and ask if they ever collect payment at the time of the sale (a cash sale), they respond in the affirmative.

What's the problem?

Here's the answer:

When this happens, it's almost always due to the fact that the user is selecting **Receive Payments** from the Customers menu or the Home Page.

The Receive Payments transaction is for receiving payment on an existing invoice, and automatically posts a credit to Accounts Receivable.

When you have a cash sale, you must use the Sales Receipt transaction (Customers | Enter Sales Receipts).

There are other ways to create an unwanted credit accidentally, but 90% of the time, the problem is caused by using Receive Payments when no invoice exists.

Returning a Security Deposit

A reader wrote to find help with a problem. She takes security deposits from tenants, and posts them to an Other Current Liability account. When she has to return the security deposit she issues a credit memo, and chooses the option to create a refund check. She says that each customer record shows multiple entries for these transactions.

A credit memo is a credit against currently owed balances (or is held, awaiting future invoices). That description doesn't fit the return of a security deposit, so it's an inappropriate transaction type. To return a security deposit, use the Write Checks window to write the check and post it to the Other Current Liability account.

Turning a Retained Customer Credit into a Refund

We receive quite a few requests for help that are similar to a message that arrived this week: "I need to refund a customer for overpayment on their account. I issued a credit memo and chose the option to retain the credit. Now I want to issue a check to the customer instead, because I probably won't get orders from this customer in the future. Do I have to void the credit and then create a new credit so I can choose Refund?"

No, you can change the credit from a Retained Credit to a Refund quite easily.

1. Press **Ctrl-J** to open the Customer Center.
2. Select the customer or job in the Customer & Jobs pane on the left.
3. Double-click the Credit Memo listing (in the right pane) to open the credit memo.

4. When the transaction window opens, click the icon at the top of the window labeled **Use Credit To**. The same dialog you saw when you created the credit appears

Available Credit

This credit memo or refund has a remaining balance which you may use.

What would you like to do with this credit?

- ○ Retain as an available credit
- ● Give a refund
- ○ Apply to an invoice

OK

5. Select **Give A Refund** and click **OK** to open the Issue A Refund dialog box.

Issue a Refund

A refund is due to	Accounting Systems Plus:software	Issue this refund via	Check
Refund Amount	$ 60.00	Account	100000 · Operating ...
Date	02/07/2016 Ref/Check No. To Print	Ending Balance	125,763.48
Address	Accounting Systems Plus	Class	
Memo	101011		

☑ To be printed

OK   Cancel

6. Fill in the Class and Memo fields as desired and click **OK**.

The Credit memo is stamped "REFUNDED", and the refund check is created.

CHAPTER 16:

CUSTOMER PAYMENTS TIPS

When a customer sends payment for an invoice, you record that payment. The journal for the payment (the Cash Receipts Journal) posts the transaction appropriately. Table 3-5 displays the journal for a customer payment.

ACCOUNT	DEBIT	CREDIT
1000 - Bank Account	42.80	
1100 - Accounts Receivable		42.80

Table 3-5: The invoice payment arrived and the receivables are adjusted.

It's important to understand that an invoice payment journal has no references to the accounts that are tracking income, inventory, or sales tax. All of that information was posted when the original invoice was created.

The payment of the invoice is a second and separate transaction. Many accountants receive questions from clients who want to know why the payment doesn't show what products were sold or what general ledger income accounts were affected. (Those questions are a large motivation for the writing of this book.)

–Excerpt from **Accounting Savvy for Business Owners**
by Phillip B. Goodman CPA (available at www.cpa911.com)

Posting Interest Income as Part of Customer Payments

A reader wrote with the following interesting problem: "We have several government contracts and those customers often don't pay our invoices by the due date. When payments are late they automatically arrive with additional funds to cover interest. If we enter the amount of the payment check in the Receive Payments window, QuickBooks wants us to create a credit or send a refund. Neither of those choices works. How do we post this interest?"

1. Select **Customers | Receive Payments** from the menu bar to open the Receive Payments window.

2. From the Received From drop down list, choose the appropriate customer or job.

3. Enter the amount of the original invoice (do not include the added interest) in the Amount field.

4. Select **Check** from the Pmt. Method drop down list, and enter the check number in the Check # field.

5. Be sure you're sending payments to Undeposited Funds, not directly to the bank account (if you don't see a

Deposit To field it means that QuickBooks is set to use Undeposited Funds by default).

NOTE: *To change the default settings for using the Deposit To field, choose **Edit | Preferences | Payments**, and click the Company Preferences tab. Next, check (or uncheck) the **Use Undeposited Funds As A Default Deposit To Account**. When checked, the Undeposited Funds account is used automatically and no choices are availble. When unchecked, the Deposit To field appears, enabling you to choose the account you want to use.*

---

6. If there are multiple invoices for this customer/job, make sure the correct invoice is selected for payment.

7. Click **Save & Close** to process the payment.

The next step is to deal with interest payment. If you don't already have one, create an item named Interest Paid and link it to your income account. Then create a sales receipt for the interest.

1. Choose **Customers | Enter Sales Receipts** from the menu bar to open the Enter Sales Receipts window.

2. Select the customer or job from the Customer: Job drop down list.

3. From the Payment Method drop down list, choose **Check** and enter the check number in the Check No. field.

4. Choose the Interest Paid item in the Item field.

5. Enter the amount of the additional interest added to the payment.

6. Enter a memo explaining that this is the additional interest sent with the invoice payment.

7. Click **Save & Close** to complete the transaction.

Now the invoice is paid, the interest is posted, no credits are due, and both transactions are in the Undeposited Funds account. When you're ready to deposit the check, open the Make Deposits window (Banking | Make Deposits), and select both transactions to match the amount of the deposit you're making.

Customer Payments Through a Collection Agency

A reader wrote to ask how to handle customer payments that come in through a collection agency. The customer pays the agency, which takes its commission and remits the balance. How do you pay off the invoice in QuickBooks with this reduced amount?

The first thing you need is an expense account for the collection fees. If you don't have one, follow these steps to create one:

1. Press **CTRL-A** to open the Chart of Accounts window.

2. Press **CTRL-N** to open the Add New Account dialog.

3. Select **Expense** as the account type and click **Continue** to open the second Add New Account dialog.

4. Enter **Collection Fees** (or something similar) in the Account Name field.

5. Enter a description if needed and click **Save & Close** to create the new account.

Once you've created the expense account the next step is to receive the payment.

1. From the menu bar, select **Customers | Receive Payments** to open the Receive Payments window.

2. Choose the customer or job from the Received From drop down list.

3. In Amount field enter the amount of the check received.

4. Click the **Discount & Credits** button to display the Discount & Credits dialog.

5. Enter the remaing balance (the agency commission) in the Amount Of Discount field.

6. Choose the Collection Fees expense account from the Discount Account drop down list.

7. Click **Done** to return to the Receive Payments window.

8. Click **Save & Close** to complete the transaction.

The invoice is now paid and the agency commission recorded.

Applying a Negotiated Amount to an Open Invoice

A reader wrote to ask how to handle a situation in which he negotiated a reduced payment amount for an invoice.

Don't change the invoice amount because you want to track the history behind the transaction in QuickBooks. Furthermore, if the invoice was created in a previous year, your tax return for that year won't match your records.

First, create an account named Discounts Given if you don't already have that account in your QuickBooks chart of accounts. (Ask your accountant if he/she prefers this account to be an Income or Expense account.)

Once the Discounts Given account is set up, the next step is to pay the invoice:

1. Select **Customers | Receive Payments** from the menu bar to open the Receive Payments window.
2. From the Received From drop down list, choose the customer/job
3. Enter the negotiated amount in the Amount field.
4. If there are multiple open invoices for this customer be sure to select the invoice to which the negotiated amount is to be applied.
5. Next, click the **Discounts & Credits** button, move to the Discount tab and apply the unpaid balance to the discounts account.

6. This clears the unpaid portion of the invoice, and the invoice has no open balance.

Applying Partial Payments to QuickBooks Line Items

We get hundreds of letters each year from users who want to apply partial payments from customers to specific line items. They sell multiple items, e.g. Item A for 100.00, Item B for $50.00, Item C for $25.00; this creates an invoice in the amount of $175.00. The customer sends $100.00 to pay for Item A. QuickBooks merely records a partial payment for the amount, and there's no way to link that payment to Item A. Quite a few of these correspondents complain that QuickBooks should be criticized for this "lack."

Cmon' folks, this is silly. We don't hesitate to criticize QuickBooks for badly designed or missing features, but applying a partial payment without regard to line items is normal behavior.

Let's say you have a department store charge account and buy a couch for $2000.00 and a chair for $700.00. When you send a payment of $2000.00, do you think the store's software is noting that the chair remains "unpaid for"? Nope, the store's software merely notes that you still owe $700.00.

Do any of your credit cards track the items you're paying for when you send a partial payment that matches a specific item? Nope. And their accounting software is even more sophisticated (and more expensive) than QuickBooks.

Applying Payments to Multiple Jobs

We receive many queries from readers about the correct way to apply customer payments that pay off invoices for multiple jobs in QuickBooks. Of course, the term "correct" means different things to different people.

At cpa911.com, we define "correct" as the solution that makes it easy to track what you did, and makes reports accurate and easy to understand. Therefore, the correct way to apply customer payments for multiple jobs is to select one job at a time in the Receive Payments window.

However, when we respond with these instructions we often get another message from those readers, telling us that others (especially the self-proclaimed experts in the QuickBooks Community Forums) advise receiving the payment by selecting the customer in the Receive Payments window and checking off the individual jobs for which the customer sent the payment.

The results of each method are different, and we care about those differences. To illustrate, we'll go over both methods for a customer that has two open invoices, and each invoice is for a separate job. In this example, we're using the customer named AAA.

Enter a Separate Transaction for Each Job/Invoice

This customer sent a check for $405.00, which is the total of two invoices for two separate jobs. To apply the payment to the individual jobs/invoices use the following steps:

1. Choose **Customers | Receive Payments** from the menu bar to open the Receive Payments window.
2. In the Received From field, select one of the jobs (do not select the customer).
3. In the Amount field, enter the amount of the check that is earmarked for this job's invoice. In this example, the check is for $405, but we're using it to pay two separte job invoices.

4. Enter the check number.

5. Select the appropriate invoice if there are multiple open invoices for this job.

6. Click **Save & New**.

7. In the Received From field, select another job with an invoice covered by this payment and repeat these steps.

Each transaction uses the same check number, of course. Make sure you send payments to Undeposited Funds, not to a bank account. When you select the multiple payments in the QuickBooks Make Deposit window, the deposit total is equal to the amount of the check.

If you need to check this customer's status (perhaps the customer has called to discuss his account), here's what you'll find in QuickBooks:

- Selecting a job in the QuickBooks customer center displays the invoices, payments, and current balance for that job.

- When you create a QuickReport on the job, the invoices and payments are displayed.

- When you create a QuickReport on the customer, the invoices and payments are linked to the appropriate jobs.

Enter a Single Transaction for All Jobs/Invoices

To enter a single QuickBooks transaction for payment of multiple invoices linked to separate job, use the following steps:

1. Select the customer instead of a job in the Receive Payments window (QuickBooks displays all the open invoices for all jobs).

2. Enter the amount of the check.

3. Enter the check number.

4. Select all the invoices paid by this check.

Save the transaction and use the Make Deposits window to move the payment to the bank account.

If you need to check this customer's status (perhaps the customer has called to discuss his account), you'll find the following:

- Selecting a job in the customer center displays the invoices, but not the payments.
- When you create a QuickReport on a job, only the invoices are displayed.
- When you create a QuickReport on the customer, the invoices and payments are not linked to the appropriate jobs; instead, the payments are linked to a job named "Other."

You may have saved thirty seconds of time when you created the payment transaction, but your accounting records for jobs aren't accurate. This is NOT the way to track customer activity in QuickBooks.

Customer Payment Sent to Wrong Company

A reader wrote with the following question: "I run two separate companies and there are a few customers who do business with both companies. I received a check from a customer who had an invoice from Company 1, but made the check payable to Company 2. I don't want to return the check and wait for a new payment, but my bank won't let me deposit this check into the company in which the customer has an open invoice. I want to deposit the check, and then write a check to the other company. How do I do that?"

Create an account named InterCompany-Exchange. It can be an Other Current Asset, Current Liability, or Income account; it doesn't matter because the account will always have a zero balance. In fact you might want to create this account in both companies in case the same thing happens the other way around.

1. Select **Banking | Make Deposits** to open the Make Deposits window. If the Payments To Deposits window opens click **Cancel** to ignore existing payments and move to the Make Deposits window.
2. Choose the appropriate bank account in the Deposit To field, and enter today's date.

3. Use the From Account drop down list and select the new InterCompany-Exchange account you created.

4. Enter a memo explaining what you're doing, and fill in the rest of the fields with the relevant information.

5. Click **Save & Close** to complete the deposit transaction.

You could also use a journal entry, debiting the bank account and crediting the account you created to exchange money.

The next step is to get the money to the correct company.

1. Press **CTRL-W** to open the Write Checks window.

2. Select the bank account into which the original check was deposited.

3. In the Pay To The Order Of field, enter the name of the sister company (add it as an "Other Name.")

4. Enter the amount of original check.

5. Move to the Expenses tab and select the InterCompany-Exchange account.

6. Add a memo explaining the transaction.

7. Click **Save & Close** to create the new check.

Now, open the sister company QuickBooks company file to apply the check to the correct customer invoice. In the other company, open the Receive Payments window, select the customer or job, and use the new check to pay the appropriate invoice.

If you take a look at the InterCompany-Exchange account in the original company file, you'll see that the transactions washed, and the account balance is zero.

Multiple Payment Methods for a Single Invoice

A reader wants to know how to enter a customer payment when the customer pays part of the amount due in cash or by check, and the rest with a credit card. The credit card payment won't be part of the deposit she makes (she has to wait until the money is transferred to the bank by the merchant card bank), so she needs separate deposit amounts to make bank reconciliation work properly.

1. Choose **Cutomers | Receive Payments** from the menu bar to open the Receive Payments window.

2. Select the customer in the Received From drop down list.

3. In the Amount field enter the total of the credit card payment.

4. Select the credit card type from the Pmt. Method drop down list.

5. Enter a note in the memo field such as "Partial payment via credit card."

6. Only enter the full credit card number if you have turned on the QuickBooks Customer Credit Card Protection feature.

> *NOTE: You should only retain credit card information if you believe the customer will be reusing the card in the near future, AND if you have enabled the QuickBooks credit card security feature. To do so, choose **Company | Customer Credit Card Protection** from the menu bar, and click the **Enable Protection** button in the dialog that appears. Then fill in the rest of the information as needed.*

7. If your preferences are not set to make the Undeposited Funds account the default Deposit To account, select **Undeposited Funds** from the Deposit To drop down list.

> *TIP: To make the Undeposited Funds account the default Deposit To account, select **Edit | Preferences** to open the Preferences dialog. Click the **Payments** icon in the left pane, and the **Company Preferences** tab in the right. Then enable (place a check mark in the box) the **Use Undeposited Funds As A Default Deposit To Account** option.*

8. If there are multiple open invoices, select the correct invoice.

9. Select **Leave This As An Underpayment**.

10. Click **Save & New** to save this payment and open a new Receive Payments window.

In the new window, select the same customer and repeat the earlier steps. However, this time enter the amount paid by cash or check and indicate the appropriate Pmt. Method. Finally, click **Save & Close** to complete the transaction.

The next step is to make the deposit.

1. Choose **Banking | Make Deposits** to open the Payments To Deposit window. In addition to any other pending deposits you may have, you'll see the two just made for the invoice paid using multiple payment methods.

2. Select the one made by cash or check and click **OK**.

3. In the Make Deposits window, choose the Deposit To account, enter the date and a memo if desired, and click **Save & Close** to complete the deposit.

You can deposit the credit card payment in a separate Make Deposits window when the funds have been transferred to your bank.

CHAPTER 17:

ESTIMATES TIPS & TRICKS

Estimates are a necessity for contractors, and creating an estimate in QuickBooks is a straightforward process. Choose Customers | Create Estimates to open the Create Estimates transaction window.

Enter the customer, item, and financial information, including a markup if you're using markups. QuickBooks calculates the total. When you print the estimate for your customer, only the total amounts appear; any cost and markup rates you entered are not printed.

If the job has phases (for instance a demolition phase, then a building phase, then a finishing carpentry phase, and finally a cleanup phase), you should think about creating separate estimates for each phase. This makes progress billing less complicated, and also provides a way to track estimated-to-final costs on a phase-by-phase basis (which is valuable information to have when you create an estimate for another similar job). In addition, if you subcontract any of the phases, it's easier to track the subcontractor on a specific phase and estimate.

–Excerpt from **Running QuickBooks 2012 Premier Editions**
by Kathy Ivens and Tom Barich (available at www.cpa911.com)

Adding a Signature Line to Estimates

A number of readers asked how to add a signature line to their QuickBooks estimates where customers can sign to indicate approval. Any of the estimate templates can accommodate this; all you have to do is enable it.

1. Select **Customers | Create Estimates** to open the Create Estimates window.

2. From the Template drop down list, choose the estimate template you want to modify. For this example we'll use the Quote template.

3. Click the small down arrow next to the Customize button on the template toolbar, and select **Manage Templates**.

4. In the Manage Templates window that opens, click **OK** to open the Basic Customization window.

5. Now click the **Additional Customization** button to open the Additional Customization window. In the case of our example template, the Quote template, a dialog appears, explaining that this is an Intuit template that cannot be modified.

NOTE: All QuickBooks templates can be modified using the Basic Customization window. It allows changes to fonts, colors, and basic header information. For more complex customizations you must use the Additional Customization window. Templates designed to be used with QuickBooks preprinted forms cannot be modified in the Additional Customization window. Therefore, QuickBooks offers to make a copy which can be modified.

6. Click the **Make A Copy** button to create a copy of the Quote template that can be modified, and to open the Additional Customization window.

7. Click the **Footer** tab to display options for the template footer.

8. Place a checkmark in the Print check box next to the Signature field. If you look at the preview in the right pane you'll see that the signature line has been added to the bottom of the template.

9. If you wish, change the text from Signature to something more descriptive, such as "I agree (sign and date)."

You can use the QuickBooks layout designer to move the signature line to the left or center of the form, or to shorten the line-item section of the form to provide more space for the signature. Simply click the **Layout Designer** button at the bottom of the Additional Customization window.

No Batch Printing for Estimates

A reader wrote to ask how to print all the 45 estimates he'd created in one session, the way he does when he creates invoices.

This can't be done in QuickBooks. You must print each estimate separately. You can, however, send estimates in batches by email.

Tracking Vendors for Estimates

A reader wrote to us with the following question: "When I create an estimate, the prices are based on the price I got from a particular vendor. How can I create the estimate so it records that vendor for me somewhere? Then, when the customer approves the project, I'll know which vendor to use."

The easiest way to do this is to customize the Estimate template and use the Other field that's available.

1. From the menu bar, select **Customers | Create Estimates** to open the Create Estimates window.
2. Choose the template you want to modify from the Templates drop down list.
3. Click the down arrow to the right of the Customize button and select **Manage Templates** to open the Manage Templates window. If you want to use a different estimate template, choose it from the Select Template list.

4. Click **OK** to open the Basic Customization window where you can make minor changes to fonts, colors, and header information.

5. Now click the **Additional Customization** button to display the Additional Customization window.

NOTE: *If you've selected an Intuit template that is used with preprinted forms you'll have to make a copy before proceeding.*

---

6. Click the **Columns** tab to display the options for the main body of the estimate.

7. Place a checkmark in the boxes next to the Other 1 field and type **Vendor** in the Title field.

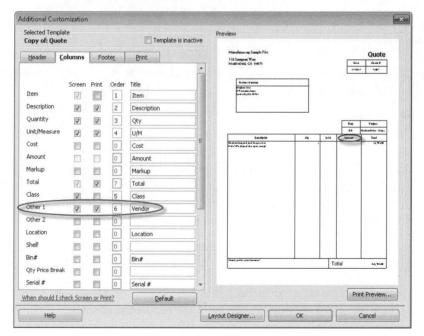

8. Continue clicking **OK** until you are returned to the Create Templates window with the now modified estimate.

9. Fill out the estimate and include the vendor name in the new Vendor column.

The only drawback to using the Other fields is that they do not appear on reports. For this reader, that did not seem to be a concern. However, if you need the new information to appear on reports the solution is simple. Either create a custom field called "Vendor" in the customer records or use one of the other fields not already in use and change the Title to Vendor.

One last thing. You can change the position of the new field by changing the number in the Order box. A lower number will move it to the left and higher number to the right.

Create Estimates Without Adding a New Customer

A reader wrote to ask how to manage estimates for potential customers. He doesn't want to add a customer unless the estimate is accepted and the potential customer becomes a real customer.

NOTE: Intuit introduced a (potentially) handy feature called the Lead Center in QuickBooks 2012 that should have resolved this problem. Unfortunately, it doesn't. While you can use it to track leads and later convert them to customers, it does not allow you to create estimates (or any other transactions) until the lead has been converted to a customer.

Fortunately, the workaround for this is rather simple.

1. Press **CTRL-J** to open the Customer Center.
2. Press **CTRL-N** to open a New Customer blank record.
3. Enter **Potential Customer** (or use some other name that indicates the status of the not-yet-a-customer) in the Customer Name field.
4. Click **OK** to create the new customer.

While you could create individual estimates using this customer and changing the name and address to reflect the name and address of each new lead, a cleaner solution is to create a new job for each new lead.

1. Press **CTRL-J** to open the Customer Center.

2. Right-click the Potential Customer listing in the Customers & Jobs pane and select **Add Job** from the menu that appears. A blank New Job record form opens.

3. Enter the lead's name as the Job Name.

4. Make sure Potential Customer appears in the Customer field.

5. Fill out as much or as little information as needed.

6. Click **OK** to save the new lead or click **Next** to create another.

Now you're ready to create estimates for your new leads.

1. Select **Customers | Create Estimates** to open the Create Estimates window.

2. Choose the appropriate Potential Customer job from the Customer:Job drop down list.

3. Fill out the estimate as needed.

4. Click **Save & Close** to save the new estimate.

If the lead becomes a customer you can change the job to a customer by moving the job listing to the left in the Customer & Jobs pane. If the lead does not become a customer you can remove it from the Customer Center. Since QuickBooks will not allow you to delete a customer or job as long as there are transactions connected to it, you must first delete the estimate(s) for the lead. Once the estimates have been removed you can then delete the lead (job).

Tracking Progress Invoicing

A frequent question from readers is, "How do I track the invoices against estimates, including the line items on the invoices"?

You have two ways to do this.

To track progress invoicing for a specific estimate, open the estimate and click the History icon at the top of the transaction window. All of the invoices linked to the estimate are listed and you can open any individual invoice to see the line items.

Transaction History - Estimate				
Estimate Information				Cancel
Customer:Jobs	Retail Homeowners:Custom Orde...			Help
Estimate Date	12/15/2016			Print
Estimate No.	71009	Estimate Total	18,000.00	
Memo				
Sent Date		Send Method		
Invoice line items				Edit Estimate
Type	Date	Number	Amount	Est. Balance	Go To
Invoice	12/15/2016	71104	-4,500.00	13,500.00	

To track progress invoicing for a group of estimates, choose **Reports | Jobs, Time & Mileage | Job Progress Invoices vs. Estimates**. You can modify the report to filter by date range, customer, or any other criteria. Then double-click each listing to drill down to the details.

CHAPTER 18:

INVENTORY TIPS & TRICKS

An inventory item is a physical product you manufacture or purchase for the purpose of reselling to a customer. The main types of businesses that track inventory are manufacturers, wholesale distributors, and retailers. If you drop-ship to customers from a manufacturer or distributor, you don't track inventory because it's not your warehouse that's being tracked for inventory quantities and value.

Things you buy to sell to customers in the normal course of business with those customers usually aren't tracked as inventory. This means that if you're an electrician and you buy wire, outlets, and various electrical parts that you sell to your customers as part of a job, you usually don't have to track those parts as inventory. On the other hand, a contractor with ten trucks, each carrying $10,000 in supplies/parts, might have to report inventory. If you fit that definition (or the amount of stock you have on trucks and/or in a warehouse comes close to that definition), ask your accountant if the amount still in stock at the end of the year is significant enough to add inventory to your tax return.

–Excerpt from **Accounting Savvy for Business Owners**
by Phillip B. Goodman CPA (available at www.cpa911.com)

Include Shipping in Item Price

Several readers have asked how to include shipping in a QuickBooks item price in a way that doesn't show shipping as a separate line on the sales transaction form. However, they want their P & L reports to show the item income and shipping income separately.

You can do this by creating a Group in QuickBooks. For this example we'll assume you do NOT have either the sales item or the shipping item set up in QuickBooks.

Begin by creating the sales item (let's call it Gadget).

1. Select **Lists | Item List** from the menu bar to open the Item List window.
2. Press **CTRL-N** to open the New Item dialog and select Inventory Part, or Non-Inventory Part (you probably won't be shipping a service item).
3. Enter the name for this part and any other pertinent data.
4. From the Account drop down list choose the appropriate sales income account.

5. Click **Next** to open another New Item dialog box so you can create the shipping item.

6. Choose **Other Charge** from Type drop down list and enter the appropriate information.

7. Select the shipping income account from the Account drop down list.

8. Click **Next** to open a blank New Item dialog in which to create the group item.

9. Click the small down arrow next to the Type field and choose **Group** from the drop down list that appears.

10. Enter a group name that is clearly describes the function of the group. The reason for this is that the group name will not appear on the printed sales draft, only the group description.

11. In the Description field enter the text you want to appear on the printed transaction form.

12. Leave the **Print Items In Group** option unchecked so that only the group item (description) prints on the transaction form.

13. In the table at the bottom of the dialog select the items to include in the group.

When you create a sales transaction (either an invoice or a sales receipt) the items included in the group will appear on the screen version of the transaction form. That's when you can enter the shipping fee. However, when you print the form, only the group description will appear on the printout.

Providing a Discount for Purchase of Multiple Items

A reader wrote to say he has three items for sale, and wants to be able to give a discount to any customer who buys all three items at the same time. He couldn't figure out how to automate this process. He's using QuickBooks Pro, so assemblies aren't available, but even if he switches to a Premier Edition he said he didn't want to tie up inventory by creating assemblies that would be sold infrequently (when you create assemblies the individual items are immediately removed from inventory and become part of the assembly).

The solution is to create a Group item, which means inventory isn't decremented until you sell the group.

1. Select **Lists | Item List** to display the Item List window.
2. Press **CTRL-N** to open a New Item dialog box.
3. From the Type drop down list select **Group**.
4. Enter a name for the Group. It doesn't appear on printed sales forms so you can use it more as a description for your own reference.
5. Enter the text you want to appear on the final form in the Description field. Only the description appears on the printed form
6. If you want only the group to appear on the printed transaction form leave the **Print Items In Group** option unchecked. To have all the items appear on the printed form check the option.
7. In the table at the bottom of the dialog add all the items to be included in the discount. You can even include a subtotal item after the other items have been added, and then a discount item to discount the subtotal.

8. Click **OK** to create the new group.

When you add the group item to a sales transaction each item in the group appears on the transaction regardless of the status of the Print Items In Group option. That option only affects the printed form.

TIP: If you plan to include all the items in the group on the printed sales form, be sure that all items included in the group have a description. Only the item descriptions and the group description appear on the printed transaction form. Therefore items in the group without descriptions will only display the quantity and price, and nothing else on the printed form (see the fig following this tip).

We Do It All
1234 North 14th Street
Philadelphia PA 19100

Sales Receipt

Date 2/15/2016
Sale # 36

Sold To

Jerry Adams
1213 Mapleview Dr
Philadelphia, PA 19101

Ship To

Check #
Payment Method

Ship Date 2/15/2016
Due Date   2/15/2016
Other

Description	Qty	Rate	Amount
	1	20.00	20.00
	1	160.00	160.00
	1	50.00	50.00
			230.00
Wholesale Discount		-10.00%	-23.00
Gadget Pak			207.00

If you don't want to include the subtotal and discount items in the group you can add them to the sales form after the group item. Another advantage to a group item is that you can use it even if you're not tracking inventory.

Changing the Inventory Adjustment Account Type

When you enable inventory tracking, QuickBooks automatically adds accounts: an Inventory asset account and an Inventory Adjustment expense account.

Many accountants prefer the Inventory Adjustment account to be of the account type Cost of Goods. Check with your accountant before you create a new Inventory Adjustment COG account, and if he or she thinks it's a good idea, don't forget to create a Journal Entry to transfer inventory adjustments you've posted to the expense account into the COG account.

When you use the COG Inventory Adjustment account, QuickBooks displays an error message telling you that inventory adjustments should be posted to an expense account (if inventory is decremented) or an income account (if inventory is increased).

We've queried many accountants and never found one who agreed that an increase in inventory is an increase in income, and we've always wondered where Intuit found the accountant who advised them on that message (it's probably the same accountant who told Intuit to add Political Contributions as an expense account in the chart of accounts Quick-Books used to offer when you set up a new company, which is, of course, a totally illegal deduction - fortunately, they've since removed that one). Ignore the message, and select the option to stop displaying the message in the future.

Assemblies Vs. Group Items

A reader wrote to ask why the individual components in the assembly items he created weren't decremented from inventory when he sold an assembly. He pointed out that before he used assemblies, he'd used group items, and the individual components were removed from inventory upon the sale of a group item.

QuickBooks decrements the components of assemblies (which are only available in QuickBooks Premier editions) when you build the assembly. Thereafter, the assembly is a discrete inventory item, and the assembly item itself is decremented when you sell it.

NOTE: Assemblies are only available in QuickBooks Premier Editions. If you are using QuickBooks Pro, you are limited to using Group items to sell multiple items in a single package.

A group is not a discrete item; it's a virtual collection of components that continue to be treated as individual components when you sell the group. You don't pre-build groups, so the components are decremented when you sell the group.

Tracking Cost of Goods for Give-Away Inventory

A reader wants to send inventory items to customers as samples, and asked us how to do this because she's not sure what is supposed to happen to cost of goods. She wanted to know whether an inventory adjustment or a journal entry is the right approach.

You have a cost of goods sold posting for inventory, whether you charge for the inventory, give it away, or sell it below cost. It's useful to track the freebies you provide to customers as samples or incentives, so the best way to decrement the inventory count, and post the cost of goods sold, is to create a sales receipt. Just put zero in the amount column.

TIP: *If you don't want to track samples for potential customers (who are not yet on your Customer List), create a customer for this purpose. At CPA911 Publishing we have a customer named House, and we use it to ship review copies of our books. We enter a Sales Receipt for zero dollars, and we enter the name and address of the recipient. When QuickBooks asks if we want to save the name and address information we entered on the customer record (for the customer named House), we click **No**. However, we can look through the Sales Receipts to see where we sent books.*

Work in Process Inventory

A reader wrote to ask how to handle the purchase of inventory items that are improved and changed before they're sold to customers. He creates purchase orders for the original products and additional purchase orders for the improvements (subcontractors who perform additional work on the base product). He wants to know if there's a way to have QuickBooks automatically convert the two items into one inventory part and total the cost.

QuickBooks lacks a real Bill of Materials module (even in the Premier editions that offer assemblies - although upgrading to QuickBooks Premier and using assemblies might be a solution for this user).

NOTE: *The solution we use is an accounting procedure, not a QuickBooks procedure, so check with your accountant before implementing this.*

Begin by creating a new inventory item for the finished product.

1. Select **Lists | Item List** to open the Item List window.
2. Press **CTRL-N** to open a New Item dialog.
3. Choose **Inventory** from the Type drop down list.
4. Enter a name for the finished product (the original product plus the improvements)
5. Enter the appropriate Description, Rate, and Tax Code information.
6. From the Account drop down list, select the income account to which sales of this product will be posted.
7. Click **OK** to create the new inventory item.

Next, create a new account to keep track of the new and improved items.

1. Press **CTRL-A** to open the Chart of Accounts window.
2. Press **CTRL-N** to create a new account.
3. Move to the Other Account Types drop down list and select **Other Current Asset**.
4. Click **Continue** to open the Add New Account dialog.
5. Enter an account number in the Number field if you're using account numbers.
6. In the Account Name field enter **WIP Inventory** (WIP stands for Work In Process).

7. Enter a description such as Work in Process Inventory.

8. Click **Save & Close** to add the new account.

TIP: *Don't use purchase orders. (If the vendor requires a P.O., create one in a word processing application.) When the bills arrive for the original products (which are not in your Item List) and the improvements, post the transactions to the WIP Inventory account.*

When the finished products are ready, use an Adjust Quantity/Value on Hand transaction to bring them into inventory.

1. Select **Vendors | Inventory Activities | Adjust Quantity/Value On Hand** to open the adjustment window.

2. Choose **Quantity And Total Value** from the Adjustment Type drop down list.

3. From the Adjustment Account drop down list select the **WIP Inventory** account.

4. Move to the table and choose the finished inventory item from the Item drop down list.

5. Tab to the New Quantity field and enter the quantity of finished items. If you already have some finished items on hand enter the new qantity in the Qty Difference field.

6. Move to the New Value field and enter the total of the bills for the original item plus improvements. If you already have some of the finished product on hand, add the new total cost to the Value you'll find at the bottom left of the Adjust Quantity/Value On Hand window.

7. Click **Save & Close** to process the adjustment.

If you check the WIP Inventory account in the Chart of Accounts window you'll see that the new inventory value has washed the amount of the original bills for the products and the improvements.

Backflushing Inventory in QuickBooks?

A reader asked whether it's possible to set QuickBooks up for backflushing inventory for their assemblies. The answer is "No."

For those who aren't familiar with the term backflushing, it's an inventory practice that helps avoid tying up too much money in inventory. Backflushing software tracks inventory needed for building products from existing inventory parts (called Assemblies in QuickBooks) and when products are built, the software automatically orders replacement products.

TIP: Although QuickBooks won't automatically reorder replacement products for you, it will alert you when your on hand quantity of items reaches a certain point. In the inventory item record, enter the number of items to trigger the alert in the Reorder Point field. Then choose **Edit | Preferences | Reminders | Company Preferences** to display QuickBooks reminders. Set the Inventory To Reorder option to either **Show Summary** or **Show List** depending on how much detail you want in the alert.

Actually, good backflushing software tracks history and trends, and then predicts need with amazing accuracy. When the software is properly configured, you're never short of product, and you're never carrying unnecessary inventory (which means you're not tying up cash). Backflushing features are found in high-end accounting software applications (usually quite expensive). This type of software is not generally found in small businesses, it's for major manufacturing companies.

Using Inventory for Warranty Repairs

A reader wrote to ask how to manage the use of inventory items when they're used to repair products under warranty. Her accountant told her to use an invoice and a matching credit memo for warranty work. However, she noticed that the inventory quantity wasn't being decremented.

Actually, it was being decremented by the invoice, but then put right back by the credit memo. Consequently, it was a wash, and the end result was that no inventory was being removed.

When you issue a credit the item is put back into inventory and the cost of goods sold isn't recorded. If you create an invoice, even if you change the amount of every line item to zero, the inventory is removed and the COGS is applied.

The best way to do this is with a zero-amount invoice to the customer for whom you're making the repair.

1. Press **Ctrl-I** to open the Create Invoices window.
2. Select the customer from the Customer:Job drop down list.
3. Enter the inventory item(s) used for the warranty work.
4. Move to the Rate field for each item and change the amount to zero.
5. Enter **Warranty work** or something similar in the Memo field.
6. Click **Save & Close** to create the zero-amount invoice.

Tracking Inventory Reorder Points

A reader wrote to say that she has a lot of inventory items, but only needs to worry about reorder points for a few of them. She can't find a QuickBooks report that shows her only the items that have reorder points configured. When she runs an Item Listing report, she has to scroll through all the items, and make notes in order to track those with reorder point information.

It takes a customized report to get the information she needs. The easiest way is to start with an Item Listing report.

1. Choose **Reports | List | Item Listing** to open the report.
2. Click the **Customize Report** button (Modify Report in pre 2012 versions).
3. In the Display tab, deselect extraneous information in the Columns list. Usually, you only need the item, the reorder point, and the quantity on hand. You may also want to include the description, quantity on p.o., and the preferred vendor.
4. Move to the Filters tab and choose **Item** from the Filter list.
5. From the Item drop down list choose **All Inventory Items**.
6. Go back to the Filter list and select **Reorder Point**
7. Select the Greater Than option (**>=**), and enter **.01** in the text box.

8. Click the **Header/Footer** tab to view the options for the report header and footer.

9. Change the Report Title to **Reorder Point Report** or something similar.

10. Click **OK** to save the changes and return to the report.

The report no longer displays items that don't have reorder points. Memorize the report (press **CTRL-M**) so you don't have to go through the customization effort again.

Inventory Valuation Report Problem

A reader wrote to tell us that he ran an inventory valuation report, along with other sales reports, for his accountant. The accountant told him that he believed there was a problem with the inventory valuation because the numbers didn't make sense when compared to the sales reports. The reader asked us for help, because he couldn't figure out where any error could have been introduced. He didn't modify or customize any of the reports.

We suspected the culprit was inactive items since the inventory valuation report displays information for active items only. We asked him to try the following:

1. Select **Lists | Item list** to open the Item List window.

2. Enable (check) the **Include Inactive** option at the bottom of the window.

3. Locate any inactive items that had a quantity greater than zero and make them active by removing the X to the left of the item name.

4. Rerun the inventory valuation report. Sure enough, the report matched the totals his accountant was looking for.

Sometimes users make items inactive, even if there's stock left, because they don't want to sell the item at the moment. Unfortunately, the QuickBooks inventory valuation report doesn't include inactive items, even if stock exists (nor does the report have an option to include inactive items with existing stock, which is a serious flaw). Because inventory that exists has value by the very fact of its existence, the QuickBooks inventory valuation report should be renamed Inventory Valuation of Active Items, or the report should be fixed to match accounting rules and expectations.

Accrued Inventory Transactions Display in Cash Basis Reports

We've had many messages from users asking why they see unpaid expenses in reports they've configured for Cash Basis. The answer is that QuickBooks displays unpaid vendor bills for received inventory, and unpaid customer invoices for inventory. Inventory based companies that run cash basis reports won't see accurate "pictures" of the company's financial status without these balances showing.

When you create an invoice, a journal of the transaction must be created (it's a Sales Journal), so the postings can be transferred to the general ledger. The transaction is posted to all the affected accounts. If you're using accounting software, this is automatic, and many software users don't understand how the journal assigns the transaction to accounts.

As a business owner, you should understand how transactions are posted; otherwise, the data in reports can be confusing. The following examples are presented to clarify the way invoices are journalized as they feed the general ledger.

The journal for a simple sales transaction, involving no inventory or sales tax is shown in the following table. The posting to Accounts Receivable represents the total amount of the invoice.

ACCOUNT	DEBIT	CREDIT
4000 - Income		100.00
1100 - Accounts Receivable	100.00	

If you post certain types of sales to different income accounts as you create the individual items covered by the invoice, the journal for the invoice tracks those income accounts as well.

ACCOUNT	DEBIT	CREDIT
4010 - Income for Services		60.00
4020 - Income for Products		40.00
1100 - Accounts Receivable	100.00	

–Excerpt from **Accounting Savvy for Business Owners**
by Phillip B. Goodman CPA (available at www.cpa911.com)

Printing Invoices in Alphabetical Order

Several readers have written to ask how to print batches of QuickBooks invoices in alphabetical order (using the customer name). They print sheets of labels in alphabetical order and want to pull the invoices from the printer and insert them in the envelopes. Most of these correspondents indicated that they created invoices over multiple days and print them at the end of each week.

Unfortunately, QuickBooks has no user sort options for invoices. It's probably best to create the invoices alphabetically and then print each invoice as you create it. From our testing we've determined that Quick-Books apparently sorts first by date, then by invoice number

Using QuickBooks Estimates for Installment Invoicing

A reader wrote to ask how to set up installment invoices in QuickBooks for customers who buy his services but want to pay off the total price in four installments. He said he was going to create an invoice for the total and accept partial payments, but that means he has to print statements to remind customers of the balance due.

While you can create separate QuickBooks invoices with the appropriate due dates, a simpler way would be to create an estimate and invoice 25% of the total at a time.

> **NOTE:** To use this method, Progress Invoicing must be enabled in QuickBooks. To enable it, select **Edit | Preferences | Jobs & Estimates | Company Preferences**, and set the Do You Do Progress Invoicing option to **Yes**.

1. Choose **Customers | Create Estimates** to open the Create Estimates window.
2. Enter the Customer:Job, all the necessary items, and click the **Save** button on the window toolbar.

3. Now, click the **Create Invoice** button on the window toolbar to open the Create Progress Invoice Based On Estimate dialog box.

4. Select the **Create Invoice For A Percentage Of The Entire Estimate** option and enter **25** in the text box.

5. Click **OK** to create the new invoice for 25% of the total.

Memorized Invoices Don't Update Price Changes

Readers write to complain that when they update an item price their memorized invoices don't automatically pick up the new price. When they have a hundred or more memorized invoices this is a real problem.

You have to define the word "memorized" literally. A memorized invoice is frozen, the data that's in the invoice when you memorize it doesn't ever change. If you have a great many invoices to send to the same customers each month, memorizing invoices for every customer works as long as nothing changes (the item price, the terms, the customer's address, and so on).

If your memorized invoices contain items that are likely to change periodically, consider using a third-party add-on for automatically creating invoices. You can find add-ons at http://marketplace.intuit.com/.

We recommended an excellent invoice creation program from Karl Irvin (a developer we rate highly and never hesitate to recommend) to a client who runs a condominium association and they've been extremely pleased with it.

Unlike memorized transactions, you don't have to create a transaction for every single customer being invoiced; instead, a "model" invoice is automatically applied to all customers you select, and all the data (current price, current terms, current billing address, etc) is applied when you generate the invoices. You can learn more about this application at Karl Irvin's website at http://www.q2q.us/idoverview.htm.

Using Line Item Discounts

We frequently receive queries from readers about the proper method for giving a discount on a specific customer's invoice in QuickBooks. Usually the reader wants to know how to discount the goods or services provided and avoid giving a discount on shipping.

Here's the rule to remember: When you enter a percentage discount item on a line, QuickBooks automatically takes the discount against the amount of the line above the discount item. If you're selling one item, enter that item and then enter the discount item. Enter the shipping charge on the line after the discount item.

| | | | | TERMS | DUE DATE |
| | | | | Net 15 ▼ | 12/30/2016 🗔 |

ITEM	DESCRIPTION	QUANTITY	RATE	AMOUNT	Tax
Door Frame	standard interior door frame	2	150.00	300.00	Tax
Discount	10% Discount		-10.0%	-30.00	Non
Delivery Charges	Freight & Delivery		40.00	40.00	Non

If you're selling multiple items in QuickBooks and want to discount all of them, enter all the items and then enter a Subtotal item. On the next line, enter the discount item (which applies the discount to the subtotal because that's what's on the line above the discount). Then use the next line to enter the shipping charges.

				TERMS	DUE DATE
				Net 15 ▼	12/30/2016 📅

ITEM	DESCRIPTION	QUANTITY	RATE	AMOUNT	Tax
Door Frame	standard interior door frame	2	150.00	300.00	Tax
Hardware:Bra...	standard interior brass hinge	6	20.00	120.00	Tax
Hardware:Doo...	Standard Doorknobs	2	30.00	60.00	Tax
Subtotal	Subtotal			480.00	
Discount	10% Discount		-10.0%	-48.00	Non
Delivery Charges	Freight & Delivery		50.00	50.00	Non

Enforcing Customer Credit Limits

We receive a lot of queries from users who want to know how to enforce customer credit limits in Quickbooks. QuickBooks doesn't support enforced credit limits; instead, the software issues a warning when an invoice will exceed the limit. Users are free to ignore the warning.

Enforcing customer credit limits in QuickBooks is a matter of setting rules for employees. You can also make some changes to the customer's configuration to make the credit limit problem more apparent: Create a Terms option named NO CREDIT (all caps makes it more noticeable on the Invoice template) and assign it to customers who are close to or over their credit limits. Change the name of the customer to add the words NO CREDIT or NO INVOICES to the customer name, e.g. SmithCo-NO CREDIT. (The customer name doesn't appear on any transaction forms.)

Turning Off Credit Limit Warnings

A reader wrote to ask how to turn off the warning that a customer is over the credit limit when creating an invoice for that customer. He said he doesn't really use the credit limit, and would like to stop the warnings.

There isn't a preference for disabling the credit limit warnings, because QuickBooks assumes you don't want to keep selling to customers who don't pay their bills (a rather logical assumption). If you don't use the credit limit feature for its intended purpose, remove the credit limit amounts from the customer records, because that's the only way to turn off the warning.

1. Press **CTRL-J** to open the Customer Center window.
2. Double-click the customer name in the Customers & Jobs pane to edit the customer record.
3. Click the **Payment Info** tab to view payment options for this customer.
4. Delete the amount in the Credit Limit field.

NOTE: Do not enter zero in the Credit Limit field. Leave it blank. If you enter zero, QuickBooks will consider every invoice greater than zero to be over the credit limit, thus making the alert situation even worse.

5. Click **OK** to save the change.

Correcting Duplicate Invoices

A reader wrote to say he'd inadvertently created two invoices for the same sale. The invoices were dated several months ago. The customer paid one invoice this month. If he voids the extra invoice, it changes his accounting totals for the period ending two months ago, which he doesn't want to do. He wants to know how to fix the problem so it only affects the numbers for this month. (This is even more urgent if the months crossed a fiscal year.)

The solution is to issue a credit memo with the current date. When QuickBooks asks if you want to apply this credit to an existing invoice, select the duplicate invoice.

Tracking E-Mailed Invoices

A reader wrote to say that she loves the ability to e-mail invoices to customers, and she uses the batch e-mail feature to send all the invoices she's created. However, this feature lacks the paper trail she used for printed invoices. She used to print invoices to a dot-matrix printer that held carbonless duplicates, and she filed the duplicate copy.

The solution is simple. Mark each invoice both **To Be Printed** and **To Be E-Mailed**. You can batch print them first, and then e-mail the same batch. To make it even more efficient, print the batch to the PDF995 printer that is automatically installed with QuickBooks. That way all the printouts are sent to a single PDF file that can be stored on your hard drive and easily backed up.

Invoicing with Group Items

A carpenter wrote to say that he preferred to send simple, one-line, invoices to his customers. He works out the cost of materials and labor and enters that total on the invoice. He wanted to know whether that total-only item should be set up as a Service or an Other Charge type.

It doesn't matter which item type he uses, but he's missing the chance to track the way he makes his money.

Tracking the total for materials he buys against materials he invoices is important. Tracking his labor charges is also important as he analyzes his income. The number of hours he's working to garner his labor income may be revealing (maybe it's time to hire somebody or hire subcontractors to boost labor income).

The best way to manage "one-line invoicing" is to create a Group Item named "Charges", or "Total Labor & Materials" that includes an Item named Materials (which is linked to one income account) and another Item named Labor (which is linked to a different income account).

When you create the group, do NOT select the option labeled Print Items In Group (the option is available in the Group Item dialog). Deselecting that option tells QuickBooks to combine the amounts into one line with the total amount when you print the invoice for the customer. Be sure to include a description for the group item, since only the description appears on the printed invoice and not the group item name.

When you create the invoice, you see each item in the group on its own line in the Create Invoices window. Fill in each item's amount to get the grand total.

When you print the invoice, the individual lines you filled out won't appear; only the description you created for the Group Item and the total amount appear on the printed invoice.

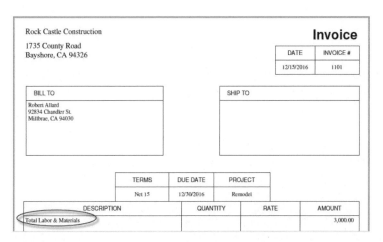

Customer Wants Special Shipping

A reader asked us how to manage shipping to a customer who wants shipping to be charged directly to the customer's UPS account (the customer provided the account number).

This means that shipping is not supposed to be included on the invoice. The problem is that the person entering the invoice doesn't always remember that this customer wants direct shipping charges. The reader wants to know whether there's a way to stop the entry of shipping charges on invoices for certain customers.

There's no way to configure any customer so that shipping charges won't "take" on an invoice. However, you can create a visual memory stimulator. Create a Ship Via listing named UPSCollect or UPSDirect. When this entry appears on the Create Invoices form, it reminds you to ship this order via UPS (even if you normally use another shipper), and it also reminds you to skip the shipping charges in the invoice. The Ship Via entry can be up to 15 characters, which should be enough to handle these situations.

Create Multiple Memorized Invoices En-Masse

A reader wrote to ask if there's a shortcut to creating multiple memorized invoices en-masse. He sends retainer invoices to 35 clients each month, and each of the invoices has been memorized. He opens them one at a time to create the new invoice, print it, and mail it.

Create a Memorized Transaction Group for the invoices that you send on the same date. Name the group appropriately (e.g. Retainers). Creating all the invoices at once is a snap.

1. Press **CTRL-T** to open the Memorized Transaction List.
2. Double-click the group for which you want to create the invoices. This opens the Using Group dialog box.

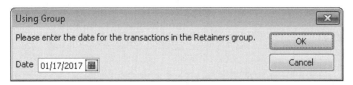

3. Set the transaction date for the invoices in this batch.
4. Click **OK** to create invoices for all the group members.

Creating a new memorized transaction for the group is easy. In the Memorize Transaction dialog select the option **Add To Group**, and then select the group from the Group Name drop-down list.

To move existing memorized transactions into the group, open the Memorized Transaction list, select the transaction listing and press **CTRL-E** to edit the transaction. Select the option **Add To Group**, and then select the group from the drop-down list. The transaction's listing is indented under the Group listing in the Memorized Transactions List.

TIP: You can drag existing transactions to the right to indent them, which automatically makes them members of the Group that's listed above the transaction listing.

Invoicing Multiple Jobs in One Invoice

We've had many queries about preparing an invoice that covers multiple jobs. One person said he managed real estate properties and the owner wanted one invoice for the repair expenses on all properties (each property is a job in QuickBooks). Another person said he had a customer who insisted on receiving one invoice a month, with all jobs listed (each job is a specific project).

You can't combine multiple jobs in one invoice in QuickBooks. However, since both of these queries involved monthly invoices, there's a workaround in the form of Statements.

Create the invoices on a job-by-job basis, but don't print them or send them to the customer. Then, at the end of the month, create a statement covering that month's activities. The invoices listed on the statement are grouped by job (although they're not subtotaled by job).

This is more effective if you create a customized template for the statement (in fact, use the title Monthly Activities or something similar instead of the title Statement). You can also eliminate the aging fields in the footer to make it look more like an invoice.

Invoicing From Separate Divisions

A reader wrote with the following question: "I have 3 classes setup to track different "Doing Business As" companies that are run under my corporation. Each DBA has its own set of customers and I've designed invoices that are different for each DBA. My problem is that the invoice numbering is sequential, which makes it hard to track each DBA's outstanding invoices. Is there a setting where I can set invoice numbering based on Class?"

The answer is no. However, there is simple solution to the problem. Create a separate A/R account for each DBA. Each A/R account uses its own sequential numbers.

Of course, this means that you have to remember to select the appropriate A/R account every time you create an invoice or receive a payment.

Invoicing Monthly for Daily Services

An attorney asks, "How do I track my time on a daily basis and then send my client an invoice at the end of the month? I don't want to send my client six invoices if there were six days that month in which I performed work for him."

Select **Customers | Enter Time | Time / Enter Single Activity**. Fill out a single activity time sheet for each task performed.

Create an invoice at the end of the month and choose **Select The Outstanding Billable Time And Costs**...option to open the Choose Billable Time And Costs window. From the Time tab select the activities to include on the invoice.

Un-hiding Reimbursable Expenses

We get this question frequently: "While preparing invoices, I selected "Hide" for some reimbursable expenses. Now I want to invoice the customer for the expenses, but I can't figure out how to "un-hide" those costs."

Hide means delete or remove (Intuit really should change that text). Hiding billable costs removes them from the customer record as billable costs, but the link to the customer in the original transaction line is not removed, so the information still appears for job costing purposes.

If you change your mind, and want to invoice the customer, open the original vendor transaction and put a check mark in the Billable column. The next time you prepare an invoice, the reimbursement is available.

If you don't want to include the costs in the invoice you're currently preparing, but plan to include the costs in a later invoice, don't hide them, merely skip them; they'll remain so you can use them in a future invoice.

How to Avoid Accidental Billable Costs

Many users link a job to an expense in order to do job costing, and don't want to invoice the customer for the expense. QuickBooks automatically selects "Billable" when you enter a customer or job in the Enter Bills or Write Checks windows, and sometimes you may not remember to deselect the billable check mark. That means your job costing reports are wrong, and it also means that when you prepare an invoice for a customer with an accidental billable cost you'll be surprised by a message asking if you want to add your accumulated billable costs to the invoice.

Before you create job costing reports, and/or before you begin invoicing customers, do a last-minute check to see if any expenses were inadvertently marked "Billable."

1. Select **Reports | Jobs, Time & Mileage | Unbilled Costs By Job** to run the Unbilled Costs By Job report.

2. Double-click each transaction and find the checkmarks in the Billable column.

3. Deselect the check mark for those expenses that are not to be billed, and save the transaction.

4. When the report has no erroneous listings, it's safe to run job costing reports and create invoices.

Then, use the Feedback command on the Help menu to tell Intuit there should be a Preference setting for whether costs linked to jobs should default to Billable or Not Billable.

Sending Information to Vendors for Drop Shipping

A reader asked for help in streamlining his order process for drop shipping. He said he created an invoice for the customer, and then typed an order for the same items and sent it to the vendor who drop ships the products. He wanted to make this faster by sending a copy of the invoice to the vendor but he doesn't want the vendor to see the prices he's charging his customers.

The solution to this is a Packing Slip, a template built into Quick-Books. While the packing slip is designed for your warehouse personnel (who also have no business knowing what you're charging your customers), it will work perfectly for drop shipping.

1. Create, save, and print the invoice.

2. With the invoice still open, move to the Template drop down list and choose **Packing Slip**.

3. Print the Packing Slip. While the onscreen version of the packing slip still shows the prices, the printed version does not.

Invoice Printing Problem

A reader sent e-mail that started with, "Help, I'm going crazy trying to send invoices." Here's what happened. He usually sends invoices weekly, but on this particular week his assistant created the invoices and printed them. All of the invoices printed incorrectly, with a very large top margin (almost 2" deep).

The same thing happened when he voided and re-created the invoices. He tried using the Layout Designer but it didn't work. He opened another company file, and he also opened a sample company file, but the same thing happened. If he prints to another printer, including a PDF converter printer, the large top margin is always there. He verified the file and everything is fine.

The most common reason for this problem is that somebody selected "Letterhead" as the paper type for printing invoices (instead of Blank Paper). QuickBooks moved everything down to make room for the pre-printed letterhead. The change could have been made in any company file, including a sample company file. Once a printer setup is changed in any company file, the change is replicated to all company files because QuickBooks configures printers for the entire installation of the software instead of individual company files (which we think is a preposterous and unwise way to design accounting software).

To fix the problem reset the printer settings.

1. Select **File | Printer Setup** to open the Printer Setup dialog box.

2. From the Form Name drop down list choose the form for which you want to change the printer settings. Invoice, in this case.

3. Make sure the Printer Name and Printer Type are correct.

4. Move to the Print On section and select **Blank Paper**.

5. Click **OK** to save the printer settings.

Part II

CHAPTER 20:

PAYROLL TIPS & TRICKS

Net pay is the amount of the paycheck an employee receives and it's the gross pay less the deductions. The amount of money deducted from employees' paychecks might stay in your bank account (albeit not for long) but you can't spend it because it isn't your money. These are your payroll liabilities and you have to remit the money to other entities.

NOTE: Net pay isn't posted to any payroll expense account; instead, it's posted to the bank account you use for payroll (as a check or as a direct deposit).

In addition to the money withheld from employees' checks, there are other payments related to payroll you have to send to other entities (covered in the following sections of this chapter). These are your payroll expenses.

NOTE: The money you spend on an outside payroll company isn't a payroll expense, it's an operating expense.

When you post your payroll, net pay is posted to the bank account. It's a credit to the bank account because it reduces the bank account balance. Table 9-1 is a simplified (actually, oversimplified) view of the way net pay is posted...

ACCOUNT	DEBIT	CREDIT
Salaries & Wages	5000.00	
Deductions from paychecks		2100.00
Bank account		2900.00

–Excerpt from **Accounting Savvy for Business Owners**
by Phillip B. Goodman CPA (available at www.cpa911.com)

Printing Blank Timesheets

Several users have asked how to print a blank timesheet in QuickBooks. They want users to fill out the forms and then have the bookkeeper transfer the data to a QuickBooks timesheet. To print a blank timesheet, click the arrow to the right of the Print button and select **Print Blank Timesheet**.

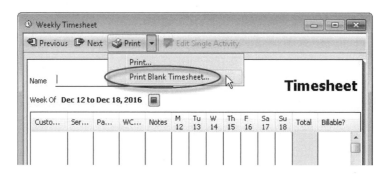

Employee Missing in QuickBooks Payroll

We've had several queries from users who had made employees inactive in QuickBooks and are now bringing those employees back. All of the e-mail we received related the same problem: "I deselected the Employee **Is Inactive** check box, but when I run payroll the employee isn't listed."

This invariably turns out to be an employee who left the company for one reason or another. For such employees, it's not enough to make the active again by removing the Inactive check mark. You also have to remove the Release Date from the employee record.

1. Select **Employees | Employee Center** to open the Employee Center window.
2. Choose **All Employees** from the View drop down list in the Employees pane to view both active and inactive employees.
3. Double-click the employee you want to reinstate.

4. From the Change Tabs drop down list, select **Employment Info**.

5. Delete the Release Date field info.
6. Deselect (remove the checkmark) the **Employee Is Inactive** option.
7. Click **OK** to save the changes.

Now the employee will show up when you run QuickBooks payroll.

How to Skip an Employee Deduction for a Loan

A reader wanted to know how to change the setup for an employee deduction against a loan so that it could be eliminated for a single paycheck in QuickBooks.

You don't change the setup for the deduction, you merely eliminate it from the paycheck. Edit the paycheck details in QuickBooks to remove the deduction or to change the amount to 0.00.

Third Party Disability Payments

We had several messages from users who wanted to know how to prepare W-2s for employees who have received disability payments from the insurance company. The insurance company sends W-2s to the employees for those payments, and the users wanted to know which box, if any, of the company W-2s should reflect those payments.

If the insurance company sends a W-2, the company W-2 for that employee does not contain any reference to the amounts paid by the insurance company. However, "sick pay" types of insurance payments should be added to Form 941 (line 7B).

Entering Year to Date Payroll Information

An accountant who helps her clients set up QuickBooks payroll wrote with a long litany of complaints about the payroll setup process. She wanted to know whether there's a way to enter the year to date payroll information she has, without using the payroll setup feature, and without entering each paycheck for each employee.

Many accountants and users have written to complain that the QuickBooks payroll setup is hard to use, goes on forever, and sometimes disappears or displays other strange and buggy behavior before you finish (it takes most people more than one day to complete the entire setup and the secret to continuing smoothly is to avoid issuing any payroll checks until you've finished).

Here's an undocumented shortcut for entering year to date payroll information:

1. Create the employees (which you can do without running Payroll Setup).
2. From the menu bar, choose **Help | About QuickBooks** to display the product information window.

3. Press the keyboard combination **CTRL-SHIFT-Y** to launch the Set Up YTD Amounts wizard.

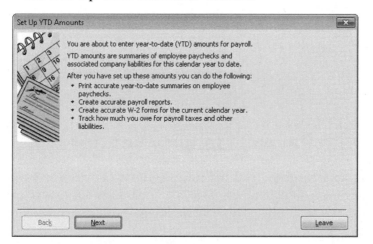

4. Continue through the wizard and enter all necessary payroll information for each employee.

In addition to employee information, the wizard also provides the opportuntity to enter payments previously made for payroll liabilities.

Remember that you can set up your payroll items, and everything else involved with configuring payroll, without using the Payroll Setup feature.

Federal Payroll Remittances

A reader wrote to complain that she didn't see a Federal payroll liability in the Payroll Liabilities window.

That's because there isn't an entity called "Federal Liabilities." You must select Federal Withholding, FICA (both employer and employee), and Medicare (both employer and employee). When you configure these payroll items, they all need to have the same Vendor so QuickBooks will create one check for the total amounts.

Part II

The vendor is the bank in which your payroll account exists (if you write checks and use coupons), or the IRS if you make your payments online.

CAUTION: If you're remitting 940 (FUTA), don't include that with your regular federal liability payment (which is a 941 payment). The 940 requires its own coupon and check.

Setting up Payroll Liability Vendors

When you create your payroll liability vendors, use vendor names that match your needs, such as 941, 940, etc. In the vendor configuration window, put the actual name of the payee (your bank) in the field labeled Print On Check As.

This makes the vendor name a vendor "code", which is the name you use when setting up vendors for payroll items. That way, you can select the 941 liabilities (all of which are linked to the vendor named 941) and the 940 liability and QuickBooks will print separate checks.

Payroll Garnishment Collection Fees

Some government agencies are offering a fee to employers who collect garnishment amounts from employees. The fee is recognition of the work it takes to set up and collect garnishments (which can be quite complicated). A reader who does her payroll in QuickBooks couldn't figure out how to remit the garnishment check, because she's supposed to take her fee out of the garnished amount.

- Set the garnishment up as a payroll item, posting it to a payroll liability account you establish for this purpose, and linking it to the appropriate vendor.
- Set up an Income account for the fee.

Click the **View/Pay** button in the Pay Scheduled Liabilities window to review and create the check. When QuickBooks displays the check, enter the fee as another line item in the check, posting it to the Income account you created, and making sure you use a minus sign for the amount. The net check is sent to the vendor/agency, and the fee income is posted properly.

Timesheet Payroll Item Column Missing

A reader asked what would cause QuickBooks to omit the Payroll Item column from one employee's timesheet, while showing that column for all other employees.

The only possible reason is that this employee is not configured for creating paychecks through timesheets.

1. Select **Employees | Employee Center** from the menu bar.
2. Double-click the employee name in the Employees pane to edit the record.
3. Choose **Payroll And Compensation Info** from the Change Tabs drop down list.
4. Check the **Use Time Data To Create Paychecks** option.

5. Click **OK** to save the modified employee record.

When you return to the timesheet, the Payroll Item column should be visible.

Re-issue a Lost Paycheck

A bookkeeper wrote to tell us that an employee accidentally destroyed a paycheck. To make it more complicated, the paycheck was the last paycheck for the quarter, and the liabilities for the month and quarter had already been paid. The bookkeeper voided the original paycheck, and created a new one for the original date. Now, the liabilities are showing up again, awaiting payment.

You can't manage the replacement of paychecks the same way you manage the replacement of lost or destroyed vendor checks. It's more complicated than that, but if you follow these step-by-step instructions, it's easy to accomplish this task.

1. Do NOT void the original paycheck.
2. Choose **Lists | Other Names List** from the menu bar.
3. Press **CTRL-N** to to open a New Name dialog.
4. Use a variation of the employee name in the Name field, because you can't have duplicate names in your company file (e.g. Dan T. Miller becomes Daniel T. Miller).

5. After you save the new name, Press **CTRL-W** to open the Write Checks window.
6. If you have a separate payroll bank account, select it from the Bank Account drop down list.
7. From the Pay To The Order Of drop down list, choose the new "Other Name" name.

8. Enter the NET amount of the lost check and post the check to any expense account (e.g. Misc expenses).

9. Print the check, write down the check number, and give the check to the employee.

10. Open the bank register and find the original check (the one that was lost). Write down the check number.

11. Edit the original check and change the check number to the same number as the new check. If QuickBooks asks if it's OK to have duplicate check numbers, say **Yes**.

12. Edit the check you just wrote to the Other Name. Change its number to the old check number (the check that was lost or destroyed).

13. Now that the new check has the old number, void it.

Your records account for the used check number in the voided check, the correct check number for the check that the employee will deposit, your liabilities haven't changed, the W-2 will be correct, the Other Name listing and the expense account you used does not show a balance for this transaction.

Company Contributions to Employees Based on Hours

Some companies (especially those with union employees) have to make company contributions based on hours worked. For example, the union contract may require you to contribute a certain amount to a health and welfare fund for each hour worked.

Create a payroll item of the type "Company Contribution" (these are not deduction type items). Specify the liability and expense accounts to track the contributions (we prefer to create separate liability/expense subaccounts for each payroll item.) Configure Tax Tracking as None, and make sure no checkmarks appear on the list of taxes affected. Step through the payroll item wizard to list the hours upon which the contribution is based. Assign the payroll item to the appropriate employees to have the contribution appear automatically in paychecks. The amount owed appears in the Pay Liabilities report.

Employee Needs Both Salary and Hourly Wages

A bookkeeper wrote to ask how to handle a payroll complication. The corporation owns restaurants, and officers of the corporation are on salary. One of the officers supervises one of the kitchens on weekends and holidays and needs to be paid an hourly wage for that work. She wanted to know how to set up an employee who is configured for salary so that he can also be paid hourly wages.

The easiest way to do this is to have an hourly wage payroll item and add it to the officer's paycheck, below the salary wage item that appears automatically. QuickBooks will take care of all the computations; and won't object if there are two different types of compensation items on a single paycheck.

Part II

Direct Deposit Payroll via Your Bank

We've had a number of queries from readers whose banks offer ACH services and these readers are using that service to pay vendors. They want to use the ACH service to provide direct deposit of employee paychecks. They point out that the service is free at many banks, and even when there is a bank charge, it's cheaper than the QuickBooks Direct Deposit feature. They want to know how to set this up in QuickBooks payroll.

You don't have to make any configuration changes in QuickBooks to do this. Don't sign up for QuickBooks Direct Deposit, and don't configure the employee's record for direct deposit.

After you've obtained the necessary information about the employees' bank accounts (some banks require you to test new additions to your ACH transfers with a test transfer), use the following steps to pay employees:

1. Create your paychecks as usual.
2. Select the option to enter the check numbers manually (don't print the checks), and leave the check number blank. This makes reconciliation easier, because your statement won't have check numbers for ACH disbursements.
3. After the paychecks are created, choose **File | Print Forms | Pay Stubs**.
4. Print the paystubs (on regular letter size paper) and deliver them to the employees. If you have installed a PDF printer, you can print to PDF and e-mail the PDF files to the employees.

Remember that an ACH transfer is not immediate, and you will have to upload the ACH file or fill-in the ACH information on the bank's website (depending on the way your bank requires submission of ACH transfers) a couple of days before payday. Check with your bank to determine the time required to deposit the money in your employees' bank accounts. Note that to your bank, all ACH transfers are the same, so you don't have to separate your paychecks from your ACH vendor payments; you can do all your ACH transfers at once.

Confusion About Social Security Maximums

Several readers wrote with the same question, and the question indicates some confusion about the way Social Security works. In both cases, there was a new employee who had already maxed out on Social Security with the previous employer. One reader complained that when she tried to deselect Social Security in the employee's record, QuickBooks also deselected Medicare and she knew that Medicare doesn't max out and should continue to be deducted. The other reader said that he'd been told a "trick" to remove Social Security from the paycheck calculations without removing Medicare (the trick is to hold the Shift key when deselecting Social Security) and he wanted us to confirm that this was an acceptable approach.

Social Security and Medicare deductions in your payroll calculations do not have any relationship with other employers of any employee, whether the employee reached maximum with a former employer, or the employee has another job in addition to working for you. The employee's history outside of your company is irrelevant and none of your business. You are required to follow the rules within your company - when you hire an employee the rules start from scratch. Regardless of any marketing slogans, or the ease-of-use of QuickBooks, please remember that you should not perform accounting functions without consulting an accountant.

Payroll Liabilities Payment Got Lost

A reader wrote, "I made a 941 payment through EFTPS (using an electronic payment). The transaction didn't clear and then we received a notice that the payment was never received. I went to EFTPS and made the payment again. How do I void the original payment, which was made more than a month ago, and enter the new payment? Everything I try messes up my payroll liability totals."

You don't have to do anything; the new payment will clear the bank (hopefully). If this had been a check that got lost in the mail and you had to re-issue a check, the easiest way to handle that would be to stop payment on the first check, and then change the check number of the first check to the check number you used for the replacement check. Trying to void and re-enter payroll liabilities is a maze that's difficult to exit.

If your late payment included penalties and/or interest, enter a check (with no number) to cover those amounts, and post them to an expense account that tracks them (such as Other Expenses). When you reconcile your bank account, the second payment (the one that cleared) will be larger than the check entered in your register; to clear the payment select both the payment check and the penalties/interest check - the total will equal the new check.

Payroll Check Issued Without Deductions

A bookkeeper wrote to say that a client had given an employee a bonus check outside of the Payroll system. The employee had been entered as an Other Name, and the check was for the gross amount of the bonus. She explained to the client that a bonus is a payroll item and needs to be included in the payroll records. She asked us how to correct the error (the check had already been issued and deposited by the employee).

The easiest way to do this is to create a Current Asset account called Employee Advances. Go back to the check and edit it so it posts to this new account (instead of to the Bonus account originally used).

Create a new payroll item called Advance Repayment, link it to the Employee Advances asset account, configure it to calculate against the net pay, and apply None as the tax tracking.

Now issue a paycheck in which the net pay is the same as the original bonus check, which means you have to "gross up" the net amount. Apply the repayment payroll item to create a zero amount check. Change the check number to a code such as REPL (for replacement) or use letters instead of numbers (e.g. AAA). (QuickBooks doesn't print zero amount paychecks, but it will print a voucher for the employee's records.)

NOTE: If you subscribe to QuickBooks Enhanced Payroll, QuickBooks you'll find an Enter Net/Calculate Gross option on the Preview Paychecks window. If not, there are "gross up" calculators available on the Internet; use the text 'gross up payroll' in your favorite search engine to find one.

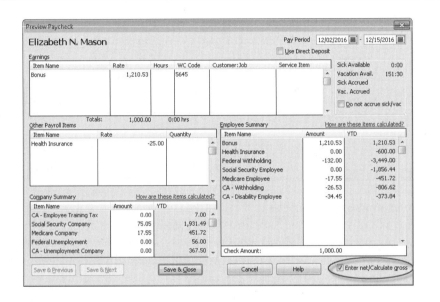

Posting Employee Contributions for Health Insurance

A reader wrote to ask for help in posting employee contributions for health insurance that are taken as payroll deductions. She has to pay the insurance bill in advance, so when she wants to remit payroll liabilities she can't write a check to clear the deductions, because the check has already been written. The liabilities total just keeps growing.

The easiest way to fix this is to change the payroll item for the deduction so it's not posting to a liability account. Instead, link the payroll item to the same account used for the check to the insurance company (an expense account). The Profit & Loss report will display the net expense for that account (the vendor payment less the credits for the employee contributions). The Vendor report shows the bills paid in full.

If you need more detail in the general ledger, make the insurance expense a parent account and create two subaccounts: Payments and EmployeeShare. Post the insurance payment to the Payments subaccount, and link the payroll item to the EmployeeShare subaccount. Your account detail reports will show the appropriate amounts and on your P & L the parent account will total the postings to the subaccounts and display the net.

Direct Deposit Stubs Display Social Security Number

A reader wrote to express his fears about identity theft as a result of the way his direct deposit stubs are printed. He works off site, his paycheck is deposited to his bank, and his employer mails him the stub. The stub prints both his social security number and his bank account number. He called the person who does payroll to complain and she told him that's how QuickBooks prints stubs, and company policy required her to mail the stubs to him.

His fears are valid, and the payroll person's statement is incorrect. QuickBooks provides several options for printing social security and bank information on direct deposit stubs.

1. Select **Edit | Preferences** and select the Payroll & Employees icon in the left pane.

2. In the My Company tab, click the button labeled **Pay Stub & Voucher Printing** to display the Payroll Printing Preferences dialog.

3. Deselect the **Employee Social Security Number** option to eliminate the full number from appearing on the pay stub.

4. If you'd like to display the last four digits of the social security number, select the option entitled **Only The**

Last Four Digitis of SSNs And Bank Account Numbers. Otherwise, deselect the option to display no social security numbers.

5. Click **OK** to save the changes and then click **OK** again to exit the Preferences dialog.

Some states require employers to print the SSN on direct deposit stubs, and if you live in one of those states, check to see whether the last four digits will suffice. If your state doesn't require this information, disable the printing of the SSN altogether.

Reimbursement for Personal Payments to 1099 Subcontractors

A reader wrote to ask for help in creating transactions for a startup business that doesn't yet have enough cash flow to support all expenses. The owner of the company is paying some subcontractors personally, and will be reimbursed when there is sufficient money. The reader creates a QuickBooks journal entry that credits the owner's equity contribution account and debits the Subcontractor expense. He enters the vendor's name on the JE lines. The 1099 report for the vendor shows zero 1099 payments.

This transaction is "washing" the vendor's 1099 payments (entering both a credit and a debit) because the vendor's name is on both lines. Enter the vendor's name only on the QuickBooks GJE line that debits the expense.

Another way to accomplish this is to create a QuickBooks liability account named "Owed to Owner" and use that instead of the equity account. In fact, if this is a corporation, a liability account named Owed to Officer is necessary (because there's no Draw or Contra-Draw account).

Paycheck Mistakenly Issued to Subcontractor

A reader wrote to ask for help. A new subcontractor was inadvertently set up as an employee, and a paycheck was issued. The subcontractor cashed the check and then called to say that the amount was too low (because of the withholding). The reader wanted to know how to fix the situation. This requires a few steps.

First, you must create the subcontractor as a vendor, but the name already exists as an employee. Edit the employee record so the employee name is different (e.g. add the letter X to the beginning of the name), and make the employee inactive.

Next, move to the Vendor Center and create the subcontractor as a vendor. Be sure to set up the vendor record for 1099 reporting if applicable (check the **Vendor Eligible For 1099** option on the Additional Info tab of the vendor record).

Void the paycheck, which also removes the liabilities attached to the paycheck. Then create a check to the vendor for the same amount (since the check was cashed). Finally, create another check for the additional money you owe the vendor.

Using Payroll in a New File

A reader wrote with the following question: "We subscribe to QuickBooks payroll, and we want to start a new file for our company. Do I have to call QuickBooks and arrange to transfer the payroll service"?

No, your subscription has a payroll service key, which will work in the new file. To get your key follow these steps in the current company file.

1. Choose **Employees | My Payroll Service | Manage Service Key**.
2. In the window that opens, select the payroll service listing and click View.
3. Write down the payroll service key.
4. Close the old company file and open the new company file.
5. In the new file, Select **Employees | My Payroll Service | Manage Service Key** to open the QuickBooks Service Keys window.
6. Click the **Add** button to open the QuickBooks Service Sign-Up wizard.

7. Type in your service key and click **Next**. Complete the wizard and return to QuickBooks.

CHAPTER 21:

SALES TAX TIPS & TRICKS

Sales tax is not income or expense, it's a liability. You're holding someone else's money (sent by your customer; but belonging to the state and/or local tax authorities), and you pass it along to the tax authorities.

Sales tax is added to the sales you generate when both the customer and the goods/services you're selling are taxable. That means that sometimes taxable goods or services aren't taxed, because the customer isn't taxable. And, sometimes a taxable customer isn't charged sales tax because the particular goods or services you sold that customer aren't taxable.

Of course, the easiest way to deal with sales tax would be to track sales tax by posting it to a liability account named Sales Tax Payable every time a sale involves sales tax, and then sending a check for the total amount in the liability account to the state. Unfortunately, it doesn't usually work that way. Most states want reports that include a lot more information than "how much tax did you collect?"

–Excerpt from **Accounting Savvy for Business Owners**
by Phillip B. Goodman CPA (available at www.cpa911.com)

Sales Tax and Budgets

A reader wrote to complain that her sales tax payments aren't showing up in her P&L Budget Vs. Actual report. She wanted to know if this is a known bug.

Sales tax is neither income nor expense; it's merely money that passes through your hands on its way to the state. It doesn't belong in a budget. Nor should there be a sales tax Expense account.

Sales Tax Not Calculating on Sales Transactions

We often receive e-mail asking why sales tax isn't being calculated for sales transactions. In order to have sales tax added to a transaction, the following configuration options must be present in the company file:

- Sales tax must be enabled.
- Both the item and the customer must be configured as Taxable.

It's possible to have a customer configured as taxable, but the item you're selling that customer may not be taxable (such as a service). In that case you won't see sales tax, because both the item and the customer must be taxable for sales tax to kick in.

To enable sales tax in your company file, follow these steps:

1. Select **Edit | Preferences** from the menu bar to open the Preferences dialog.
2. Click the **Sales Tax** icon in the left pane.
3. Click the **Company Preferences** tab to display the sales tax options for your company file.
4. Set the Do You Charge Sales Tax? option to **Yes**.

Making an item taxable is a breeze.

1. Choose **Lists | Item List** and select the item you want to make taxable.

2. Press **CTRL-E** to open the item in Edit mode.

3. Select **Tax** from the Tax Code drop down list.

4. Click **OK** to save the change and close the Edit Item dialog.

Making a customer taxable is just as easy.

1. Press **CTRL-J** to open the Customer Center.
2. From the Customers & Jobs tab, select the customer to change.
3. Press **CTRL-E** to open the Edit Customer dialog.
4. Move to the **Additional Info** tab.
5. Choose **Tax** from the Tax Code drop down list.

6. Click **OK** to save the change and return to work in QuickBooks.

Remitting Sales Tax From Previous Years

A reader wrote to say that her company had a sales tax audit and the auditor reclassified some of the non-taxable customers as taxable. Some customers have agreed to pay the sales tax they owed.

The sales tax they should have collected was from prior years, and she wanted to know how to post the receipt of payment for sales tax only and pass it through to the state without it showing as income or as a current sales tax liability. We offered the following solution, along with a reminder to show the suggestion to her accountant before implementing the procedure.

- Create an Other Current Liability account named "PastDueSalesTax."
- Create an item of type Other, called "PastDueTax" and link it to the liability account you created. Don't enter any amount for the item, because the amount will differ from customer to customer.

If you need to invoice the customers (in case they don't voluntarily send a check when you notify them of the audit results), use the Create Invoices transaction window to create the invoice, and use the "PastDueTax" item, inserting the appropriate amount for each customer. If your customers are just going to send the checks, then you can use the Sales Receipt transaction window to receive them, using that same item.

When you write the check to the state, post the check to the "PastDueSalesTax" Other Current Liability account you created. If all your customers pay you, that liability account will have a zero balance after you remit the money to the state.

If not all your customers cooperate, the liability account will have a debit balance. That amount should be moved via journal entry to an expense account that you create for this purpose (e.g. TaxExpenses). If you also owe penalties or interest to the state, you can post those amounts to an expense account named Penalties and Fines, or to the TaxExpenses account (check with your accountant).

CHAPTER 22:

TIPS FOR VENDOR BILLS

Recording a Vendor Bill

When you enter a vendor bill, the transaction amounts are recorded in a Purchases Journal, as seen in Table 4-1. In this case, the vendor bill is for an ordinary business expense, and the other side of the transaction is Accounts Payable.

ACCOUNT	DEBIT	CREDIT
6020-Telephone	205.50	
2100-Accounts Payable		205.50

Table 4-1: A typical journal for a bill for an expense.

In addition, the transaction details such as the bill number and the due date should be tracked in the vendor record (accounting software does this automatically).

Sometimes, vendor bills aren't for an expense; some banks send bills for loan payments (loans are liabilities) and other circumstances arise when you receive a bill for another type of payment. However, the majority of vendor bills are for expenses.

–Excerpt from **Accounting Savvy for Business Owners**
by Phillip B. Goodman CPA (available at www.cpa911.com)

Payment Methods: Clearing Up the Confusion

We receive many messages from readers every week on the subject of payment methods for paying vendor bills. The messages include the list of payment methods the user has created in the QuickBooks Payment Method List (DirectDeposit, DebitCard, Cash, PayPal, etc.) followed by a request for help on how to make those methods available in QuickBooks when paying vendor bills.

The payment methods you create in the list are for customer transactions only; they represent methods of receiving income. They can't be used for paying vendor bills. There are only three possible payment methods for paying vendor bills in the QuickBooks Pay Bills window:

- Check
- Credit Card (only available if you have set up your credit card as a Credit Card account in the chart of accounts).
- Online Payment (only available if you have set up online payment services with your bank and configured your bank account in QuickBooks for online payments).

Most of the time, the various payment methods you use to pay the vendor are really "checks." If you use a debit card, an automatic withdrawal by the vendor, an online payment you created on the vendor's web site, or you created an online payment on your bank's website (instead of using the QuickBooks online payment function), that's a check. It's just not a physical check, so it doesn't have a number.

Select the option labeled Assign Check No. (instead of the option "Print Checks") and leave the check number blank. Some people prefer to use "codes" for the check number, such as Debit, or DirDep, or ACH, but I leave the field blank so I don't have to re-sort the register when I reconcile the bank account (since my bank statement isn't sorted by those codes).

If you use PayPal and PayPal withdraws the money from your checking account, that's a check, too. If your PayPal account is busy and complicated (you have money flowing in both directions) and you've set up a PayPal account as a bank account, payment by PayPal is still a check, but you have to remember to select the PayPal account as the bank in Quick-Books.

Take Vendor Discounts Automatically in QuickBooks

A reader wrote to say that she gets a 2% discount when paying a bill within the stated time frame. She wants to know if there's a way to get QuickBooks to do this automatically. The answer is yes. Here's how.

1. Choose **Edit | Preferences** to open the Preferences dialog box.
2. Click the **Bills** icon in the left pane and the **Company Preferences** tab on the right.
3. In the Paying Bills section, select the option labeled **Automatically Use Discounts**.
4. Enter the QuickBooks account to which you post the discounts.

Be aware that if you don't pay the bill within the time frame but still want to take the credit (a common practice) QuickBooks won't take the discount; instead, you have to enter the credit manually from the Pay Bills window.

Tracking QuickBooks Check Numbers Linked to Vendor Bill Payments

A reader wrote to ask if there's a quick and simple way to find out which QuickBooks check number paid a particular vendor bill. If the vendor bill was paid with partial payments he needs to know all the check numbers involved.

Open the vendor bill in QuickBooks and click the **History** icon at the top of the form to view the transaction history.

Summarizing Bill Payments for Vendors

We've received quite a few requests from users who pay multiple bills from a single vendor with one check. They want to know how to include a report to the vendor showing which bills are being paid. Using the Memo field on the check doesn't work if you want to list multiple vendor invoice numbers. Some users said that a monthly check to a vendor could pay as many as 50 or more bills. One user wrote, "There has to be a better way than creating a word processing document that lists every bill being paid along with the amount for each bill."

QuickBooks can print this information for you, and you can enclose the printout with the check. After you've selected the bills to pay and created the check, perform the following steps:

1. Choose **File | Print Forms | Bill Payment Stubs**.

2. Choose the payment method used to pay the bill.

3. Select the bank account (or Credit Card) you used to pay the bill.

4. Select the check for this vendor.

5. Click **OK** to print the stub.

The resulting printout is a well-designed and easy-to-read list of the information you want the vendor to have.

Bill Payment Stub				Check Date:	12/15/2016		
				Check No.:	10080		
				Check Amount:	1,520.00		
Northpoint Construction			Paid To: Patton Hardware Supplies				
1735 County Road			4872 County Rd				
Bayshore, CA 94326			Bayshore CA 94326				
Date	Type	Reference	Original Amt.	Balance	Discount	Payment	
12/1/2016	Bill		210.00	210.00		210.00	
12/12/2016	Bill		810.00	810.00		810.00	
12/15/2016	Bill		500.00	500.00		500.00	

At the top of the form you see your company name, the check date, the check number, and the total amount of the check. Under that section is a list of all the bills paid with the check, including the Bill Date, The Original Amount, the Balance Due at the time this check was written, and the Payment Amount for each bill that's included in this check.

Replacing a Check with a Wire Transfer

A reader wrote to say that she'd printed a check to pay a vendor bill, and then accommodated the vendor's request for an electronic transfer of funds.

She tore up the check, and voided it in QuickBooks, and now the bill is appearing as unpaid. She wanted to know how to tell QuickBooks the bill has been paid, and also wanted to know what to enter in the bank register to indicate the wire transfer.

Open the Pay Bills window and pay the bill again, using the same date as the original check. Deselect the To Be Printed option, and enter EFT or WireXfer as the check number.

The important thing to learn (and remember) for the future is that instead of voiding the original check, all you have to do is replace the check number with text indicating an electronic transfer.

Unpaid Bills Report Includes a Check

A reader wrote asking if he'd discovered a QuickBooks bug, because when he ran the Unpaid Bills Detail Report one of the transactions listed was a check he'd written to a vendor.

It's not a bug, and there's only one possible reason: The check was written from the Write Checks window, and was posted to Accounts Payable instead of to an expense account (or another appropriate account).

There is never a reason to post a check created in the Write Checks window to A/P. If you're writing a check to pay a vendor bill that you entered in QuickBooks, you use the Pay Bills function (the posting was accomplished when you entered the bill). If you're writing a check for a direct disbursement (you didn't enter the bill in QuickBooks), you post the check to the appropriate account.

PO Received Quantity Vs. Amount Paid

A reader wrote that he received the items on a PO, along with a bill from the vendor. He made a partial payment on the bill, leaving a balance due. When he looks at the PO it says Received in Full. In addition, the PO doesn't show up on the Open Purchase Orders report. He wants to know why the PO is marked "In Full" and is no longer open when he hasn't finished paying for the items.

A PO tracks items that are received. This reader received all the items. The fact that there is an open balance on the bill has nothing to do with the fact that the items were received, which is what the PO tracks.

Postings for Vendor Transactions

A reader wrote to ask how to make it easier to enter vendor transactions when some of the purchases involve a two-sided item, and some are posted directly to expense accounts. He doesn't enter bills; instead, he uses direct checks. However, when he has both an item posting and an expense account posting he enters two separate bills (one for the item and one for the expense posting) in order to print a single check to the vendor.

This is unnecessary since the Enter Bills form has tabs for both expenses and items.

You can use both the Expenses tab and the Items tab in a single check or a single vendor bill. The amount of the check/bill equals the totals of both tabs.

Tracking Memos on Bills and Checks

A reader wrote to say she was careful to track transaction details by using the Memo fields on vendor bills and direct checks. However, when she runs reports on the vendors, she only sees the text from the Memo field in the header section of the transaction window (the actual check or Enter Bills form), not the text she entered in the Memo column of the line items.

The text you enter in the Memo field in the header section of a bill, or in the Memo line of a direct disbursement (Write Checks), is the text QuickBooks displays when you create a QuickReport on a vendor, the Accounts Payable account (for a bill), or the bank account (for a direct check). That text is the memo for the entire transaction.

The text you enter in the Memo column of a line item is linked to the account or the inventory item (if you use the Items tab instead of the Accounts tab) to which the line item posts. Generating reports on those accounts or inventory items displays that memo text. Because the memo text could differ for each line item in a transaction, that text isn't used for reports on vendors or the A/P and bank accounts.

CHAPTER 23:

VENDOR CREDITS TIPS

Creating a Vendor Credit

A credit from a vendor is a reverse purchase, and your transaction reflects that fact. Create the transaction using the same expense account you used when you created the original transaction, using a negative amount (a minus sign). The resulting transaction journal looks like Table 4-5.

ACCOUNT	DEBIT	CREDIT
6500-Printing		400.00
2100-Accounts Payable	400.00	

Table 4-5: This credit removes the original expense and decreases A/P.

NOTE: *If you're using accounting software, there may be a specific form for vendor credits. In that case, you probably don't have to use a negative number.*

Be sure you enter the information in the vendor record, so you can use the credit against existing or future bills. If you're using accounting software, the transfer of this information into the vendor record is automatic.

–Excerpt from **Accounting Savvy for Business Owners** by Phillip B. Goodman CPA (available at www.cpa911.com)

Can't Credit a Purchase Order

A reader asked us how to apply a credit to a purchase order. He'd ordered five items, and returned one (it was damaged). The replacement hasn't come in and he wants to know how to create a credit against the purchase order to show that an item is still expected.

You can't issue a credit against a purchase order, which is appropriate because POs aren't posting transactions.

Receive the PO and change the amount to reflect the four received items, or keep the amount for the five items, and then create a credit against the vendor bill for the returned item. To track the fact that you're awaiting an item, create another PO for that item.

Check Vouchers Missing Info on Bills Paid with Credits

We've had several questions from readers about the way check vouchers work. These readers use the vouchers to show vendors which bills are being paid with the check. For businesses that have frequent or large credits from their vendors, it isn't unusual for a vendor bill to be completely paid with an existing credit.

However, these readers complained that they cannot get that information to appear on the voucher. Bills that are partially paid by a credit are displayed on the voucher, indicating the fact that the amount due was reduced by a credit. However, the voucher doesn't display the bill numbers for bills that were paid in their entirety by credits. Therefore, the vendor doesn't know that a credit was used to pay off those bills. To make sure the vendor's records agree with their records, they have to write notes, either on the voucher, or on a separate piece of paper. They find this annoying.

Unfortunately, there's no solution, because that's how QuickBooks works; bills that are paid off totally by existing credits aren't enumerated on the voucher. If you don't want to hand-write a note, open the credit transaction you entered when you received the vendor's credit. Click the History button at the top of the Credit window, and click Print to output data that specifies the bills against which you posted the credit (including bills that were paid in full with a credit). Enclose the printout with the check you remit to the vendor.

Vendor Refunds Vs. Vendor Credits

This tip is in response to many e-mail messages with the same query. The questions all resembled this one: "I received a refund from a vendor because the vendor had made a mistake in its bill. I created a vendor credit and then deposited the money in the bank using A/P as the account and using the vendor name. The deposit showed up on my bank statement, but the credit still shows up on the vendor's record. How do I clear that credit?" (Two of the e-mail queries said the writers had made purchases with debit cards, and returned the items. Each vendor issued a credit against the debit card account. Both readers also created a credit before depositing the refund check and wanted to know how to clear the credit from the vendor record.)

There's no vendor credit involved in these transactions; instead, they are refunds, and that's a different type of transaction. Void the Credit you entered. Change the deposit so that no vendor name appears in the transaction, and post the deposit to the expense account you used when you recorded the original purchase.

If the vendor issued a credit that you recorded in QuickBooks, and then later issued a refund check to clear the credit, that transaction requires you to clear the credit with the refund check. In this case, deposit the check using the vendor's name in the Name column and posting the check to Accounts Payable. When you save the deposit, QuickBooks posts a debit (an ersatz vendor bill) to the vendor record. Open the Pay Bills window and you'll see that bill. Select it and apply the credit against it, creating a zero-amount payment. No checks are written (because Quick-Books doesn't pay zero-amount bills), the bank deposit is correct, and the credit is gone.

Debit Card Credits

Many readers are puzzled about entering credits they receive when they return a product they purchased with a debit card, and use the debit card for the credit transaction.

When you use a debit card to purchase something, you enter it as a check that has no check number (you can use a code such as DC for the check number or just leave the check number field blank).

When you get a debit card credit, the same logic applies; the money will be deposited in the bank so the transaction is a bank deposit. You can enter it directly into the bank register, or in the Make Deposits transaction window. Just enter the amount and post the transaction to the account you used when you made the original purchase with the debit card. If the credit transaction takes place after the end of the fiscal year, check with your accountant about the posting account. Your accountant may not want you to reduce the current year expense for the posting account and therefore may recommend you create an Other Income account or Other Expense account named Purchase Returns.

Note that if the purchase was for a job and you're doing job costing, the Make Deposits transaction window has a column to note the Customer:Job name - the bank register doesn't offer this field.

PART III

QuickBooks Under the Hood

CHAPTER 24:

TIPS FOR CUSTOM FIELDS

You can invent additional fields, called custom fields, for the Names lists (Customers & Jobs, Vendors, and Employees), and also for the Item list.

Custom fields are useful if there's information you want to track, but QuickBooks doesn't provide a field that fits. For example, I maintain the books for a membership-based organization, and I track member activity in QuickBooks (the membership is of a manageable size so I'm not worried about running out of room in my lists). Dues are based on the calendar year, and some members pay for several years at a time.

To track each member's expiration date, I created a field named YEAR in the Customer list. I customized the Invoice and Sales Receipt transaction templates so they include my custom field.

Each time I send an invoice, or fill out a cash receipts transaction (when I receive a membership check without an invoice), I update the YEAR field for the customer. I can create a report filtered by the current year, and send the members who appear on the report a reminder about next year's dues. For membership organizations that don't renew on a calendar year, I create a second custom field named Month.

–Excerpt from **Running QuickBooks in Nonprofits: 2nd Edition** by Kathy Ivens (available at www.cpa911.com)

Custom Field Data Not Appearing in Reports

A reader wrote to complain that although he added two custom fields to his QuickBooks customer list, and entered data for those fields in customer records, his customized A/R reports don't show the data.

QuickBooks A/R reports are for data connected to invoices. If you don't add the custom field to the invoice template and use the field in invoices, you won't see any data in reports.

Adding the custom fields to the invoice template is a simple.

1. Press **CTRL-I** to open the Create Invoices window.
2. From the Template drop down list, select the invoice to customize.
3. Click the small down arrow to the right of the Customize button on the window toolbar, and select **Manage Templates**.
4. In the Manage Templates window that opens, click **OK** to open the Basic Customization window.
5. Now click the **Additional Customization** button to access the advanced (Additional) customization options.

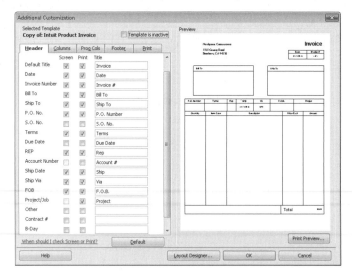

NOTE: *If you are attempting to customize an Intuit template designed for use with preprinted forms, you'll have to make a copy of the template before making additional customizations.*

---

6. On the Header tab, move down to the custom fields which are found at the bottom of the tab.

7. Check the **Screen** and/or **Print** boxes to have the custom fields appear on the onscreen form, the printed form, or both.

8. Enter the name of the field in the Title field.

9. Click **OK** twice to close both customization dialogs and return to the Create Invoices window.

You may see a message about overlapping fields. Unless you've added quite a few new fields, you can probably ignore it and click **Continue**. In the event the warning was justified, you can return to the Additional Customization window and click the **Layout Designer** button to open the Layout Designer where you can move the fields around and adjust their size to make them fit on the template properly.

Managing Delivery Routes

A reader wrote to say she has several clients that deliver goods to their customers with their own delivery vehicles, using specific routes (neighborhood locations) for each vehicle. She's tried to customize QuickBooks to produce a report of deliveries sorted by route, and has tried using Types, Items, and other built-in qualifiers on the reports, but she says it's been a real challenge to make this work.

If you create a custom field named Route for the Customer Name List, you can enter each customer's Route in the customer record, and then add the Route field to sales transactions forms (so drivers can double-check a delivery by looking at the invoice or packing slip). You can then create reports that include the Route and sort the report by Route.

To add a custom field to the customer record follow these steps:

1. Press **CTRL-J** to open the Customer Center.
2. In the Customer & Jobs pane on the left, double-click any customer to open the customer record.
3. Click the **Additional Info** tab.

4. Now click the **Define Fields** button to open the Set Up Custom Fields For Names dialog box.

5. Enter the custom field name in the Label column and check the **Cust** column to include the new field in all customer records.

6. Click **OK** to save the new, custom field.

7. Click **OK** to close the customer record.

8. Open each customer record that should contain information for this new field, and enter the information.

CHAPTER 25:

TIPS FOR CUSTOM FORMS

The default Purchase Order template (named Custom Purchase Order) is selected by default when you create POs. It lacks some fields that I consider important. However, it's quite easy to customize the template to make sure all the information you need appears on the PO. QuickBooks provides two ways to customize this template:

- *Customize the Custom Purchase Order template.*
- *Create a new customized template, with a different name, based on this Custom Purchase Order template.*

I prefer the latter approach, just because I don't like changing a basic template—instead I can keep the basic template available for other, different, customizations.

This is a two-step process: First, duplicate the default PO template and give it a new name, then customize the new template.

–Excerpt from **Running QuickBooks 2012 Premier Editions** by Kathy Ivens & Tom Barich (available at www.cpa911.com)

Problem Customizing Invoices

A reader wrote with the following problem: "I'm having a problem customizing an invoice template. When I try to make a copy of a default template so I can use it to design the new template, QuickBooks displays an error message telling me that the template can't print on letterhead. I can't make the message go away, because when I click Cancel the message keeps coming back until I force QuickBooks to close. How do I do this?"

First of all, you may not have to force QuickBooks to close. Try clicking Cancel a few more times. QuickBooks usually "gets it" eventually. If not, force QuickBooks to close and reopen it.

This message is an indication that you've set up your Invoice printing to print on Letterhead. You need to change it to print on blank paper before QuickBooks will allow you to make a copy of the invoice template.

1. Choose **File | Printer Setup** from the menu bar to open the Printer Setup dialog.
2. Select **Invoice** from the dropdown list to see the printer settings for invoices.

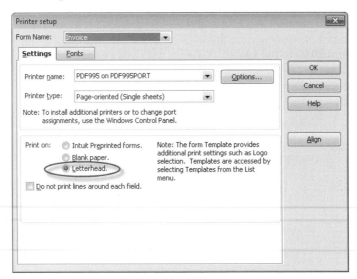

Part III

3. Move to the Print On section and select **Blank Paper**.

4. Click **OK** to save the new settings.

If you're using letterhead paper when you print Invoices, try printing with the paper set to Blank paper, and when you customize the Invoice template deselect the company name, address etc. to suppress printing of that data. Put your letterhead into the printer and see if your preprinted letterhead occupies the same space. If not, use the Layout Designer to move the fields at the top of the form to make room for your letterhead.

When you choose Letterhead as the paper choice in Printer Setup, QuickBooks starts printing the form two inches from the top of the page and shortens the size of the printing area to make up for the space it assumes your printed letterhead is using; and this creates a page length that's 9" instead of 11." Usually, this isn't necessary and you can use your letterhead with the Blank Paper selection.

Permanent Customer Message

A reader wrote to ask how she could have the customer message added to every invoice without having to select it from the drop-down list each time. She only has one customer message, but she still has to take the time to select it.

Not a problem.

1. Open the invoice to which you want to add the customer message.

2. Click the small down arrow next to the Customize button on the Create Invoices toolbar, and select **Manage Templates**.

3. With the correct invoice selected in the Select Template list, click the **OK** button to open the Basic Customization screen.

4. Now click the **Additional Customization** button to display the Additional Customization screen.

NOTE: *If you've selected an Intuit invoice that is designed to be used with Intuit's preprinted forms you will have to make a copy of the template before preceding. You can easily identifiy these templates as they usually contain Intuit in the template name.*

---

5. Click the **Footer** tab to view the footer options.

6. Move to the Long Text (Disclaimer) field and enter the customer message in the Title text box.

7. Click the **Print** checkbox to enable the printing of the customer message on the invoice.

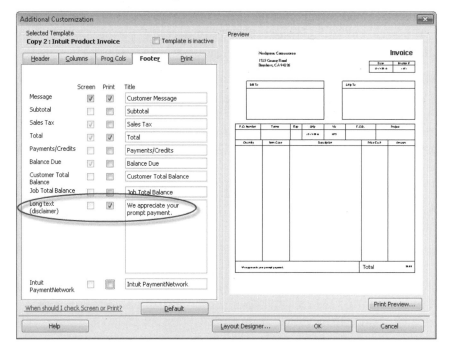

8. Click **OK** to save the changes and return to the Basic Customization screen. If you receive a message about overlapping fields you can ignore it. Unless the message is extremely long, there should be no problem.

9. Click **OK** to return to the Create Invoices dialog.

You won't see the message on the screen. However, every time you print (or Preview) an invoice the message will appear at the bottom. In addition, you can add a regular Customer Message to the invoice and it will appear above the permanent message.

Safeguarding Customized Templates

We receive frequent laments from users who tell us that a customized template (transaction form) has stopped working properly. Often, these users tell us they no longer remember all the steps they took to add fields, move fields, and so on; they don't want to face starting all over. Sometimes, the problem is that QuickBooks clobbered the template, rendering it corrupt. Most of the time, however, the problem is that another user decided to change the customization and totally messed everything up.

When you've created a customized form you can save a copy so you have a replacement if something happens to the template in your QuickBooks company file.

1. Select **Lists | Templates** from the menu bar to open the Templates list.

2. Select the template you want to save.

Name	Type
Custom Intuit Product Invoice	Invoice
Custom Progress Invoice	Invoice
Custom S.O. Invoice	Invoice
Finance Charge	Invoice
Intuit Product Invoice	Invoice
Packing Slip	Invoice
Progress Invoice	Invoice
Rock Castle Invoice	Invoice
Custom Credit Memo	Credit Memo

Templates ▾   Open Form   ☐ Include inactive

3. Click the **Templates** button and choose **Export**.

4. Select a location to store the exported template, and click **Save**.

Make sure you save it to a folder that's backed up, such as My Documents - you ARE backing up your My Documents folders every day, right? The file is saved with a .DES extension. To replace a messed-up template, use the Import command at the bottom of the Template list window to import the safety backup copy.

Changing the Text in E-Mail Messages

A reader wrote with the following question: "We changed our company name in the Company Information window, and all of the transactions and reports use the new name. However, when I e-mail forms to customers, the old name appears in the Subject field. How can I change that text?"

QuickBooks "reads" the company information and creates the text for the fields when you first set up the Send Forms feature. After that, when you send a form, the Send Forms function doesn't check the current data in the Company Information window.

It's easy to change the text.

1. Choose **Edit | Preferences** and click the Send Forms icon in the left pane.

2. Click the **Company Preferences** tab to view the e-mail message settings.

3. Change the text for each form (all the forms are in a drop-down list at the top of the dialog).

4. Click **OK** to save the changes.

Double-check the entire message to be sure you've made the necessary changes. As you can see in the screenshot above, the company name was changed in the subject line, but not in message body.

CHAPTER 26: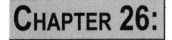
ITEMS TIPS & TRICKS

Most contractors don't need to track inventory formally, because they don't buy parts for resale the way a retail store does. Instead, they keep parts in stock for use in jobs (which is a form of resale, but not the same as running a retail parts store).

I find that many independent contractors have a long list of parts, both inventory and non-inventory, in their Item Lists. Frequently, the lists contain multiple entries of the same item.

For example, I've seen item lists in electrician's files that included Plate Covers-2hole, Plate-Covers-4hole, and so on. Plumbers have listings such as PVC-4', PVC-8', and so on. Plumbers who do this probably add a new inventory item every time they buy a different length of PVC. This is almost always totally needless, and makes the time you spend on record keeping longer than necessary.

It's much better to keep a short list of items. For example, create an item named PVC Pipe. If your customer cares about the number of feet of pipe you used, enter that information in the Description column of the invoice (I'll bet most customers don't care). Even better, use an item named Materials in your invoices, and then use the Description column to inform your customer that it was pipe.

When appropriate, use a per-unit cost and price. For example, you can have an item named Wood and enter the per-running-foot price. Then, when you use 25 feet of that wood on a job, enter the item, enter a quantity of 25, and let QuickBooks do the math.

–Excerpt from **Running QuickBooks 2012 Premier Editions**
by Kathy Ivens & Tom Barich (available at www.cpa911.com)

Payment Item is Not a Sales Item

A bookkeeper in a nonprofit organization wrote for help. She records donations in a Donation transaction window (a Sales Receipt that has been customized as a Donation form). She wrote, "When I enter a payment from a donor, it appears as a negative number, and QuickBooks won't let me save the transaction. I see an error message saying that negative sales receipts cannot be recorded. How can I prevent the donated amount from appearing as a negative number?"

The only possible explanation is that the item being used in the transaction is a Payment type item.

Payment item types are not sales items, they're used to record a pre-payment against a sale that's being invoiced, and the amount of the payment item is subtracted from the invoice total (it's like an instant credit against a balance; hence the negative number).

Create an item of the type Service or Other Charge and name it Donation or something similar. Use that item in your Donations transaction window.

Managing Inactive Items

A reader wrote to say that he has hundreds of inventory items that he no longer sells, and they're marked inactive. However, inactive items appear in the Items list in several reports and transaction windows (he cited the Adjust Inventory transaction window) and he finds it both annoying and confusing. He wants to know how to make these items "really truly inactive, because I can't delete them since they were used in transactions."

The reports and transaction windows that display inactive items do so for good reason. For example, inventory stock that exists, but which you've stopped selling, still "counts" as an asset and affects your financial status.

One trick to making it easier to tell which items are inactive is to change the item name when you make it inactive. If you change the name so it starts with a Z- or a Z-NA- (the NA means Not Available), followed by the original item name, the item appears at the bottom of the list. For example, you can change the item named Widget0555 to Z-NA-Widget0555. This makes it very easy to see which items aren't active. (QuickBooks permits 31 characters in the Item Name field, so if your existing item name has almost 31 characters you'll have to abbreviate part of the name.)

Tracking Subcontractor Rates

A reader explained that he has many subcontractors, and each subcontractor has an hourly rate. He wanted to know how to track the rates easily, and how to have the correct rate to come up automatically when he's writing checks.

If you need the correct rate to appear automatically, you have to use Items instead of posting the check to an expense account. Set up a Service Item for each contractor. Actually, it's best to create a Service Item named Subcontractors and make each subcontractor's rate a subitem (e.g. Smith,

Jones, etc), so they appear contiguously in the drop-down list when you write a check. Otherwise, you have to search for each name alphabetically in your Items list. Make sure the item is linked to the expense account you use for 1099 reporting (usually "Subcontractors" or "Outside Services").

Another method is to rename the contractor to include the rate, such as Keswick-50 if subcontractor Keswick charges you $50.00/hour. Remember that vendor names don't have to be the Payee name, because QuickBooks lets you specify the Payee name in the vendor record.

While this doesn't automatically enter the rate in the line item, it puts the data in front of you and you can easily fill out the check using the Expenses tab instead of moving to the Items tab. This is useful if you sometimes pay the subcontractor for hours (reported on the 1099) and also reimburse the contractor for materials (which is posted to the appropriate expense using the Expenses tab).

Reporting Costs and Profits of Items

A reader wrote to say she had inventory items as well as other item types. Some of the non-inventory item types are configured for costs as well as prices but she can't figure out how to get a single report that shows the costs and the profits for all items.

That information is available in the Item Profitability Report, which is available by selecting **Reports | Jobs, Time and Mileage | Item Profitability**. The report has three columns: Cost, Revenue, and Difference (the difference is the profit, of course). The report starts with Inventory items, and then lists all the other item types for which you've created items.

CHAPTER 27:

TIPS & TRICKS FOR LISTS

Lists are mini-files within your QuickBooks data file, and they contain the data you use when you create transactions. For example, the names of your customers and vendors are held in QuickBooks lists. (Database developers usually refer to these files-within-the- file as tables.)

NOTE: *QuickBooks Premier Editions have more fields and types of list entries than QuickBooks Pro, such as Assemblies as an Inventory Type, Item Price Levels, etc.*

Setting Up Your Lists

Most of the fields in the QuickBooks transaction windows require you to make a selection from a drop-down list that displays the entries you've created for the list being used in the field. If the selection you need isn't there, you can create it while you're creating the transaction (which is called on the fly data entry). However, that interrupts the process of creating a transaction, which makes you less productive. Take the time to get this basic data into your system when you first start using QuickBooks.

Creating your lists is one of those "which came first, the chicken or the egg" exercises. Some lists have fields for other list items, such as the Customers & Jobs list, where each setup window contains fields for data that's contained in auxiliary lists (Terms, Price Level, Type, and so on).

In this section, I present an overview of the lists, providing some of the things I've learned from clients and accountants about creating and using them in a productive way.

–Excerpt from **Running QuickBooks 2012 Premier Editions**
by Kathy Ivens & Tom Barich (available at www.cpa911.com)

Missing Customers

A reader wrote to say he can't find one of his customers in his QuickBooks company file. The customer name isn't displayed in the Customer Center. He can locate payments from the customer in the bank register, and he can open those payments and locate the invoice by clicking the History link on the payment. But using the QuickBooks Find feature won't locate any transactions linked to this customer. He's rebuilt the company file, but nothing helps.

We wrote back to ask him to choose All Customers in the top field of the Customer List in order to check for customers who were marked "Inactive", and sure enough, that's what had happened.

✱	Name	Balance Total	Attach
	◆House	0.00	
✱	◆Abercrombie, Kri…	0.00	
✱	◆Family Room	0.00	
✱	◆Kitchen	0.00	
✱	◆Remodel Bath…	0.00	
	◆Allard, Robert	17,603.00	
	◆Remodel	17,603.00	
	◆Babcock's Music …	269.38	
	◆Remodel	0.00	
	◆Baker, Chris	269.38	
	◆Family Room	0.00	
	◆Garage Repair	0.00	
	◆Balak, Mike	269.38	
	◆Utility Shed	0.00	
	◆Barley, Renee	0.00	
	◆Repairs	0.00	
	◆Bauman, Mark	0.00	
	◆Home Remodel	0.00	
	◆Bolinski, Rafal	0.00	
	◆2nd story ad…	0.00	
	◆Bristol, Sonya	0.00	

Customers & Jobs / Transactions — View: All Customers — Find:

This is a common occurrence, so if any QuickBooks list element is missing always check for Inactive entries. Judging from the volume of mail we receive about missing list elements, it's not unusual for the Inactive status to be applied inadvertently.

Re-sorting Lists

We've had several queries from readers about customer names appearing out of order in drop-down lists within transaction windows and in reports. Several readers told us that the customer list is sorted alphabetically in the Customer Center, but the drop-down lists and aging reports don't list customers alphabetically.

You need to re-sort the list in the Customer Center whenever drop-down lists or reports fail to list names alphabetically. The fact that the list appears in alphabetical order in the Customer Center or Vendor Center is apparently a coincidence. To re-sort the list, right-click anywhere in the Customers & Jobs tab in the left pane and select **Re-sort List**.

Find...	
Use	Ctrl+U
Refresh	
Edit Customer:Job	
New Customer	
Delete Customer:Job	
Add/Edit Multiple Customer:Jobs	
Add Job	
Make Customer:Job Inactive	
Re-sort List	
✓ Hierarchical View	
Flat View	

Using Customer Account Numbers

Our e-mail indicates that quite a few businesses use the Account Number field in the Customer Record (on the Payment Info tab). We've received many queries about sorting customer records and reports by Account Number instead of by Customer Name.

You can add a column for the Account Number to the Customer List that appears when you open the Customer Center.

1. Press **CTRL-J** to open the Customer Center.

2. Right-click anywhere in the Customer & Jobs pane and choose **Customize Columns**.

3. In the Customize Columns dialog, scroll down and select **Account No.** Then click the **Add** button to move it to the Chosen Columns pane.

4. With Account No. selected, use the **Move Up** and **Move Down** buttons to place the column where you want it. The higher the column appears in the list, the further to the left it will appear in the Customer & Jobs pane.

5. Click **OK** to return to the Customer Center.

If you need more room in the Customer & Jobs pane to see all the columns you need, drag the right side of the pane further to the right. To sort by the Account No. Column click the header once to create an ascending sort, and a second time to create a descending sort.

Many reports can also be sorted by account number, but you have to customize the report to add that column.

You cannot see the account number in drop-down lists for transaction windows. If you need that function, you must use the account number as the Customer Name.

How to Include Shipping in Item Price

Several readers have asked how to include shipping in a QuickBooks item price in a way that doesn't show shipping as a separate line on the sales transaction form. They want their P & L reports to show the item income and shipping income separately.

You can do this by creating a Group in QuickBooks.

1. Select **Lists | Item List** to open the Item List dialog.
2. Press **CTRL-N** to open the New Item dialog.
3. Choose the appropriate item Type.

4. Create the item (e.g. Gadget01, with a price of $10.00) to be sold and link it to the appropriate income account.
5. Repeat the process and create the shipping item (Other Charge type) and link it to an income account for shipping income.

6. Then Create a Group Item named Gadget and include both the Gadget01 item and the Shipping item.

NOTE: QuickBooks does not allow duplicate item names (even if one is a regular item and the other a group item). Therefore, be sure to reserve the name you want to appear on the invoice for the group item.

---

7. Make sure you leave the **Print Items In Group** option UNchecked. This will ensure that only the Gadget group item appears on the printed invoice. Both items will still apear on the screen version.

8. Use the Gadget group item in your sales transactions.

Removing Obsolete Names

A number of readers have asked how to remove obsolete customers and vendors, since QuickBooks won't let you delete a name if there are any transactions using that name in the company file. They don't want to make the names inactive (which removes the names from the drop-down list in transaction windows) because sometimes users re-activate names, and also because the names appear in some reports.

We've found the easiest way to do this is to edit and then merge the records. Change the name of one of those customers or vendors to something descriptive (such as Obsolete). Then change the name of another obsolete customer or vendor to Obsolete and say Yes when QuickBooks asks if you want to merge the records. Continue to merge until all your obsolete names are merged, and all the historical transaction records are linked to that obsolete name. (Note that when you view transactions, the information in the Bill To block remains the same, so you know the "real, original" name.)

Managing Customer Messages

A reader wrote asking how to get rid of the glut of customer messages that appear in the drop-down list of the Customer Message field on sales transaction windows. She says that users add messages constantly, and she not only wants to stop that practice, she wants to reduce the drop-down list to a few useful messages.

Customer Messages, which are stored in a QuickBooks list, can be hidden, but not deleted once they've been used in a transaction.

1. Choose **Lists | Customer & Vendor Profile Lists | Customer Message List** from the menu bar.

2. Right click the message you want to hide, and select **Make Customer Messsage Inactive** from the context menu.

That's all there is to it. The selected message immediately disappears. In the event that you decide you want the message back, check the **Include Inactive** option at the bottom of the Customer Message List dialog, right click the hidden message, and choose **Make Customer Message Active**.

Cannot Merge Profile Lists

A reader wrote to say that his company had decided to change the way they used customer and vendor Types. He wanted to know if he could merge some of the existing Types to make the change process more efficient.

You cannot merge any components in the Profile Lists (the lists that appear in the submenu when you select **Lists | Customer & Vendor Profile Lists**).

CHAPTER 28: MAINTENANCE TIPS

You can schedule automatic backups of your company file, which is the preferred method for backing up—no excuses, no waiting around the office after hours, no possibility that somebody will forget to back up your datafile.

The best time to schedule a backup is at night, when nobody is using the software. However, that plan doesn't work unless you remember the rules:

- Make sure your computer is running when you leave the office.

- If you're on a network, schedule the backup from the QuickBooks software installed on the computer that holds the company file. Make sure that computer is running when you leave the office.

- Before you leave, make sure you close QuickBooks (or close all company files if you leave the software running) because open files can't be backed up.

–Excerpt from **Running QuickBooks in Nonprofits: 2nd Edition** by Kathy Ivens (available at www.cpa911.com)

QuickBooks Scheduled Backups and the Windows Task Scheduler

Many readers have written to us to ask how QuickBooks manages to schedule automatic backups without using the Windows Task Scheduler. They don't see the QuickBooks backups when they open the Task Scheduler.

QuickBooks does use the Task Scheduler, but configures the task as "hidden." To see the status of a scheduled backup in the Scheduled Tasks window, select the option "Show Hidden Tasks."

In Windows XP the command is on the Advanced menu; in Windows Vista and Windows 7 the command is on the View menu.

Corrupted Backups On Flash Drives?

We've had a number of messages from readers who said that when they needed to restore a company file backup from a flash drive, the backup file was corrupt and couldn't be used. Now, they're stuck.

We queried a few of those readers and several admitted they don't always remember to use the Windows "Safely Remove Hardware" feature. That is almost always the cause of corrupted data on a flash drive; you can't just yank that stick out of the USB port.

That's not to say that flash drives are perfect and data can't become corrupted even if you use the Safely Remove Hardware feature. Don't rely on any single type of media for backups. If you're using flash drives, buy a separate flash drive for each day of the week so you always have multiple backups. Once a week (or, at worst, once a month) backup to the desktop (or another place on your computer) and then burn a CD and take it offsite. Look into online backup services to supplement your manual backups.

Defragmenting the Company File can Improve Performance

Like all data files, your QuickBooks company file becomes fragmented as it's opened, added to, and saved. You can see the number of fragments in your company file by pressing F2 while the file is loaded in QuickBooks.

In the Product Information window that opens, look for the entry named DB File Fragments (on the left side of the middle of the window). If the number exceeds 20, you should consider defragmenting the drive. If the number exceeds 70 you should definitely defragment the drive. (Obviously if you're on a network, it's the drive on the computer that's hosting the file that needs to be defragged.) There's no way to defragment only the company file, you have to defrag the whole drive, which should also speed up loading data files in other software.

CHAPTER 29:  MISCELLANEOUS TIPS

Planning the Class List

By the rules established for nonprofits that file tax forms, and according to accounting standards, you must track the total amount of expenses for each of the following three categories:

- *Program services*
- *Management (administration)*
- *Fundraising*

These are also the expense breakdowns that most funding agencies want to see when they consider your organization for grants. In fact, these are usually the breakdowns your board of directors wants to see.

Therefore, it makes sense to use these categories as classes (because you can create specific reports of income and expenses on a class-by-class basis in QuickBooks).

You can also create any additional classes you need. For example, many nonprofit organizations create a class for special events, and for capital improvement projects. You also need classes to track net assets (in the Equity section of your chart of accounts):

- *Restricted net assets*
- *Temporarily restricted net assets*
- *Unrestricted net assets*

–Excerpt from **Running QuickBooks in Nonprofits: 2nd Edition** by Kathy Ivens (available at www.cpa911.com)

How to Restore Loan Manager Files in QuickBooks

When users restore a QuickBooks backup (either because of a problem or as part of an upgrade to a new version), or move a QuickBooks company file to a different folder, they write to ask why they can't find their Loan Manager files. When they open the Loan Manager program, the file that loads is empty.

The QuickBooks Loan Manager runs as an add-on, it's not embedded in QuickBooks. Therefore, the Loan Manager file isn't part of your QuickBooks company file. The Loan Manager file is a separate file with an .lmr extension and it's usually saved in the same folder as your QuickBooks company file.

To restore your Loan Manager file, search your computer to find files with the extension .lmr (use *.lmr as the search criteria). You'll probably find two files with the same name in separate locations. The file with the recent date is the new, empty file that was created when you opened Loan Manager. The file with the less recent date is probably your "real" Loan Manager file. Copy the older file to the folder that has the new, empty, file and respond Yes when Windows asks if you want to replace the file. Now, when you open your QuickBooks Loan Manager, your original file, along with its data, should appear.

How to Record QuickBooks Memorized ACH Payments

A reader wrote to explain that she uses memorized transactions for monthly checks that are always for the same amount (such as rent). She has recently arranged to have some payments taken directly from the bank account. QuickBooks automatically inserts the next available check number, so when she creates the next physical check she's told the check number is already in use.

The fix is to enter **ACH** in the Check No. field of the memorized check in QuickBooks, then memorize it again and replace the original memorized check.

QuickBooks .TLG File

We get a lot of mail asking about the file named <CompanyFileName>. QBW.TLG that is housed in the folder in which you save your company file. Many users don't know what it is, but they notice the file's size, and they write to ask what it does and why it takes up so much disk space.

The TLG file can be extremely large (even larger than the company file), and it's one of the files that are backed up when you use the Quick-Books backup function to back up your company file. If you're backing up to a 2GB or 4 GB flash drive, there may not be room on that drive to hold your backup. However, the size of the TLG file is manageable; you can perform actions in QuickBooks to reduce the file size.

The Purpose of the TLG File

The TLG file is a Transaction Log file in which QuickBooks tracks changes to your data since the last time you created a verified backup of your company file. In case of an accidental data loss, Intuit Technical Support can use your transaction log file, in conjunction with your most recent verified backup, to recover your data up to your most recently saved transactions.

Deleting the TLG File

Users write to us to say that they've deleted the TLG file, and suffered no apparent problems using QuickBooks. That's true; QuickBooks automatically starts a new TLG file and the work you do in QuickBooks goes on as usual.

The problem with deleting the TLG file is that if catastrophe strikes, Intuit support personnel won't be able to reconstruct the data you entered since your last verified backup. Although it may be true that if you follow optimum procedures for backing up QuickBooks every day you'll probably never need the TLG file, it's a silly idea to risk your data by ignoring this safeguard.

NOTE: "Optimum procedures for backing up" means copying the entire QuickBooks data folder to an external source in addition to (or instead of) using the QuickBooks backup function. In addition, you must periodically test the ability to restore the data (a backup that doesn't restore isn't much of a backup).

Viewing the QBWinLog file

The QuickBooks log file is a good source of information about problems (just look for the word "Error" in the log), and support personnel often ask you to read the log or make a copy of it and send it to support (this includes support from your accountant, your IT consultant, etc., not just the "official" Intuit support staff).

The file is named qbwin.log, and the fastest way to open it is from within QuickBooks.

1. Press the **F2** key to open the Product Information window, then press the **F3** key to open the Tech Help window.
2. Move to the tab named Open File.

3. Select **QBWIN.LOG** and then click the **Open File** button to open the file in Windows Notepad, or select **Send Log Files To Intuit Support** if you've been asked to do so.

If you open the file in Notepad, you can use the Save As command to save a copy of the file in a location that's easy to find when you need it.

Fixing Printing Problems

We receive frequent queries from users who are having trouble printing in QuickBooks, even though they can print from all their other software. Either nothing happens when they select the printer and click the Print button, or the QuickBooks document prints incorrectly.

In QuickBooks, printing and printer settings are kept in a file named QBPRINT.QBP. Sometimes this file becomes corrupted. (In fact, if there's ever a contest for "the most easily and frequently corrupted file", many users tell us they think this file would be a good bet.)

To fix these problems, rename the QBPRINT.QBP file to something like QBPRINT.OLD. Then go to Print, Printer Settings and re-configure your printer (or multiple printers, if you use different printers for different types of transaction forms). QuickBooks automatically re-creates the file.

NOTE: The reason for renaming the file rather than simply deleting it is to ensure that any custom printer settings are retained in the event the file is NOT corrupt. If renaming the file doesn't solve the problem, delete the newly created file and rename qbprint.old to qbprint.qbp.

Here's where to find the QBPRINT.QBP file:

Windows XP: C:\Documents and Settings\All Users\Application Data\Intuit\QuickBooks 20xx\QBPRINT.QBP

Windows 7, Vista, or 2003 Server: C:\Program Data\Intuit\Qb20xx\QBPRINT.QBP

CHAPTER 30:

PREFERENCES TIPS

QuickBooks has a Preferences dialog in which you set accounting, transaction, and other configuration options. These options determine the display of transaction windows, the way transactions post, and what you see when QuickBooks opens...

...In this chapter, I'll cover some (but not all) of the categories in the Preferences dialog, omitting or presenting only a quick overview for those settings that are generally not important for nonprofits.

Each category in the Preferences dialog has two tabs: My Preferences and Company Preferences. Not all of the categories offer options in the My Preferences tab.

The My Preferences tab offers options that are applied when you work in QuickBooks in the currently selected company file, after logging into the file with your login name (the login name you use to enter QuickBooks, not the logon name you may be using to log on to Windows). QuickBooks remembers the settings for each login name.

The Company Preferences tab offers options for the currently opened company (QuickBooks remembers the preferences you set for each company and reloads them when you open that company file). Only the QuickBooks Admin user can work in the Company Preferences tab.

–Excerpt from **Running QuickBooks in Nonprofits: 2nd Edition** by Kathy Ivens (available at www.cpa911.com)

QuickBooks Preferences Reset During Update

A reader wrote to complain that updating to a new version of QuickBooks caused an important feature to disappear. "If I changed a customer's address when I entered a sales transaction, QuickBooks would ask if I wanted to make the change permanent. Now I don't get asked, and I have to go into the customer's record and make the change again."

This is a preference setting that apparently was changed during setup of your new QuickBooks version.

1. Choose **Edit | Preferences** to open the Preferences dialog.
2. Select the **General** icon in the left pane.
3. Click the **Company Preferences** tab to view the available options.

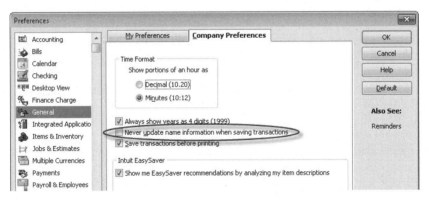

4. Deselect the checkmark next to the option labeled **Never Update Name Information When Saving Transactions**.
5. Click **OK** to save your change.

Stopping Pesky Popups

Users of earlier versions want to know how to turn off those annoying reminders that apear when you first open a company file. These aren't reminders you set up in the Reminders category of the Preferences dialog. These are messages such as "Make A Monthly Data Backup" or invitations to learn about using the QuickBooks Merchant Card Service. Clicking Mark As Done doesn't make the reminder go away permanently; eventually it returns. And, if you're an accounting firm with multiple company files, you'll be clicking Mark As Done every time you open a file when the QuickBooks internal "reminder date" kicks off these messages.

To stop the behavior you have to find the file named General.qmd and change its name to something like Generalqmd.old. (You could probably delete it, but it's always risky to delete a file connected to a software application).

In QuickBooks 2006 and earlier, the file is in the following location:

\"QuickBooksFolder"\Components\Messages

("QuickBooksFolder" means the folder in which you installed Quick-Books. By default, QuickBooks installs itself in the Program Files folder, but many people create a folder specifically for QuickBooks and use the Custom Install option to install the software in that folder.)

In QuickBooks 2007 and later, the file is in this location:

Windows XP: C:\Documents and Settings\All Users\Application

Data\Intuit\QuickBooks XXXX\Components\Messages

Windows Vista: C:\ProgramData\Intuit\QuickBooks

XXXX\Components\Messages

(Substitute the year of your QuickBooks version for XXXX, e.g. 2008.)

Bring Back Those Informational Messages

A reader wrote to say, "I don't always remember to memorize a report I've customized, and then I have to redo all the work. I must have checked the box that said I didn't want to be reminded anymore, and I want to bring that message back. How do I do that?"

1. Choose **Edit | Preferences** to open the Preferences dialog.

2. Select the **General** icon in the left pane.

3. Click the **My Preferences** tab.

4. Enable (check) the option **Bring Back All One Time Messages**.

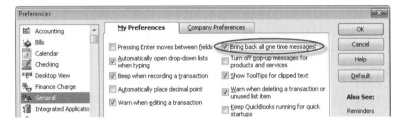

5. Click **OK**.

QuickBooks will now prompt you with every informational dialog available, and this time be more selective about the ones you turn off permanently.

Moving Through QuickBooks Windows

Several users (probably 'touch-typists' who don't like to use the mouse if they can avoid it) have asked us for a quicker way to move through the open windows in QuickBooks.

The key combination Ctrl-Tab rotates through all the open windows.

CHAPTER 31:

REPORTS TIPS & TRICKS

The balance sheet is a snapshot of your financial position at a particular moment in time. By "particular moment in time" I mean the date you choose when you create the report, which could be the current date, or the last day of the previous year, quarter, or month.

NOTE: Another term for balance sheet is statement of financial position.

The balance sheet is the primary "health record" for your business. It shows what your business owns, what it owes to others, and its equity (a combination of owners/stockholders investments and the company's profit/loss). The balance sheet has two traits you have to be aware of:

- *The word "balance" means the numbers must balance using the formula **assets = liabilities + equity**.*

- *The totals in the balance sheet reflect the entire life of your business, the numbers roll on from year to year; they don't start fresh each year. Each account displays the "net balance" of all activity in that account since Day One.*

Because the balance sheet has such important information about your company's financial health, it's usually the report that bankers want to see first when you apply for a loan.

–Excerpt from **Accounting Savvy for Business Owners**
by Phillip B. Goodman CPA (available at www.cpa911.com)

Customers with Zero Balances Appear on A/R Reports

A common question from readers is "Why are my QuickBooks A/R reports filled with transaction listings for customers that have a zero balance?"

These customers have at least one credit transaction and one unpaid invoice transaction. Even though the balance is zero as a result of the arithmetic when you add open balances and subtract credits, the transactions exist. You have to apply the credit to the invoice in the Receive Payments window and those individual transactions will no longer cause the customer to appear on QuickBooks A/R reports.

Create a Simple QuickBooks Report on Invoices

QuickBooks doesn't provide a report that displays a simple listing of invoices (Date, Invoice Number, Customer, Amount on a single line). However, you can create this report using the following steps:

1. Choose **Reports | Banking | Missing Checks** (yes, that's right, it's not a typo) from the QuickBooks menu bar.
2. Click **OK** in the Specify Account dialog that opens (it doesn't matter what bank account is displayed).
3. When the Missing Checks report opens, click **Customize Report** (Modify Report in pre-QuickBooks 2012 versions).
4. Move to the Display tab and deselect all columns except the following:
   - Date
   - Num
   - Name

- Paid
- Amount

5. Move to the Filters tab and make the following changes:
   - In the Current Filter Choices box, select the **Amount** filter and click **Remove Selected Filter**.
   - In the Filter list, select **Account** and then select your Accounts Receivable account from the Account drop-down list. If you have more than one, use the Multiple Accounts option found at the top of the drop down list.
   - In the Filter List, choose **Transaction Type** and select **Invoice** from the Transaction Type drop-down list.

6. Move to the Header/Footer tab and change the text in the Report Title field to **Invoices**.

7. Click **OK** to save your changes.

A simple list of invoices appears, and QuickBooks inserts data about missing invoice numbers or duplicate invoice numbers in the appropriate places.

Most of the missing invoice numbers aren't really missing (and therefore don't represent deleted invoices). They're usually Credit Memos, because credit memos use the same numbering sequence as invoices in QuickBooks (which is a really annoying paradigm).

If you want to see all the invoice numbers, including information about credit memos, make the following changes to the report customization:

- In the Filters tab select **Transaction Type**, choose **Multiple Transaction Types** in the drop-down list, and then select both **Invoice** and **Credit Memo**.
- In the Display tab, add the Column named Type so you know whether each line of the report is an invoice or a credit memo.

Memorize the report so you don't have to go through this again (name it Invoices).

NOTE: You can eliminate the Paid column if you really want a simple list of invoices and use the QuickBooks aging report to track unpaid invoices.

"Other" Field Missing from QuickBooks Reports

We have lots of queries from QuickBooks users who took advantage of the field named Other when they customized transaction templates. They used the Other field for a variety of things they want to track. Now they want to know how to include the text in the Other field in reports.

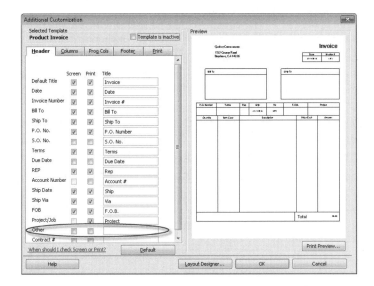

QuickBooks cannot generate reports that display data contained in the field labeled Other. Don't use this field for any information you need to use as a filter for reports, or for data you want to view on reports.

The field labeled "Other" is pretty much useless, although we've used it successfully for things you want to know when preparing a QuickBooks transaction. For example, you can insert data in the Other field to indicate whether a customer wants backorders. Have the field appear on the screen (not the printed copy) for the Invoice template. This gives you information you need to prepare the invoice, but may not be needed for reports.

If you need extra fields that will show up on reports, use custom fields instead. Open a customer, vendor, or employee record, move to the **Additional Info** tab, and click the **Define Fields** button. You can also add custom fields to items by clicking the **Custom Fields** button found in most item records.

Viewing Old Deposit Data

A reader wrote to say that her boss needed to see details about a deposit that was made many months ago. She got him the information, but then wrote with the following question: "Isn't there a faster way to do this than scrolling through a very crowded bank register, or opening the Make Deposits window and clicking Previous a million times? It took me a long time to get this information."

There sure is a faster way: choose **Reports | Banking | Deposit Detail**, and enter the date you need in both the beginning and ending date fields. Double-click the deposit listing you need and click the Print icon.

To make it even faster, here's a shortcut for entering those dates:

When you first open the report, the Dates field has the default date range (in this case, Month to Date), and the text in the field is highlighted.

Press **Tab** to move to the From field and enter the date you need with the format DDMMYY. For example, if you want the date to be November 3, 2016, type **110316** and press **Tab**. QuickBooks automatically converts the date display to 11/03/2016. Use the same pattern to enter the date in the To field. Don't forget that each component of the DDMMYY format must have two characters, so April would be entered as 04, not 4.

Unpaid Bills by Due Date

A reader wrote to say that her company pays bills every Friday, and in addition to giving her boss the checks to sign, she has to provide him with a report on the vendor bills due by the following Friday. He doesn't want to see bills that are due after that date. She can't get the report she needs by changing the date range on the accounts payable reports.

Here's how to get the right report:

1. Choose **Reports | Vendors & Payables | Unpaid Bills Detail**.
2. Click **Customize Report** (Modify Report in earlier QuickBooks versions) and move to the Filters tab.
3. In the Choose Filter list, select **Due Date**.

4. Select tomorrow's date (Saturday) in the From field, and next Friday in the To field.
5. Click **OK** to filter the report for all bills due the following Friday.

Displaying Account Descriptions in Reports

We've had a number of messages from users and accountants who find that the account names they use aren't always meaningful to people who view their reports. Many want to change the account name to the text they use in the account description, but the size limitation of the Name field doesn't permit this.

You can print the account description on reports instead of, or in addition to, the account name by turning the feature on.

1. Choose **Edit | Preferences** from the menu bar.
2. Select the **Reports & Graphs** icon in the left pane.
3. Now, click the **Company Preferences** tab to view the available options.

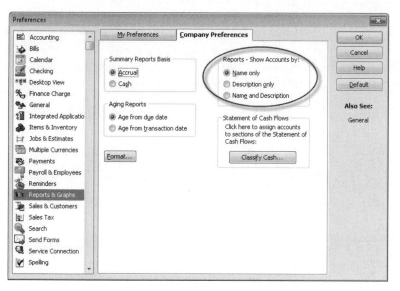

4. In the Reports - Show Accounts By section select the appropriate option (in this case either Description Only or Name And Description).
5. Click **OK** to save the new settings.

Part III

Class Information for Balance Sheet Accounts

A reader wrote to say he works for a nonprofit that uses QuickBooks and he has followed the instructions for receiving income by class, and allocating a variety of transaction types (including fund balances) to classes via journal entries. Many of the class links are applied to balance sheet accounts, but there's no way to produce a class-based balance sheet. He wants to know how he can show his Board of Directors and his grantors reports of balance sheet accounts for each program.

The best way to do this is to modify the balance sheet report by filtering for the class. You can create a report for each program, and export each report to the same Excel spreadsheet for the Board's report.

Understanding A/R Reports

A reader wrote to complain that his accounts receivable aging reports didn't make sense. Some invoices with older dates fell under the Current category, while invoices with more recent dates were listed as a month overdue. "Isn't aging linked to the date?" he asked.

Yes, aging is date-linked, but the date is not the invoice date, it's the due date, and the due date depends on the customer's terms. A customer with terms of 60 days isn't going to be "overdue" 31 days after the invoice date, but a customer with terms of 30 days is. The only way all your invoices fit neatly into overdue categories (all the dates match the overdue periods) is if all your customers have the same terms.

Adding Data and Formulas to Exported Reports

A reader wrote with the following problem: "When I export a report to EXCEL and insert a column within the exported columns, and then enter amounts in the new column, I am unable to use formulas."

We wrote back that we couldn't find a solution to this problem. Luckily, our reader had more perseverance than we did, and several hours later she sent us the following message: "I found the answer. You go to Format, click on Number and deselect the locked protection and press the F2 button - Voila! It works."

Thanks to Calista Arasaratnam for solving this problem and for taking the time to let us know the solution.

A/R and A/P Balances Showing in Cash-Basis Reports

We often receive queries from readers who don't understand why they see A/R and A/P balances when they select "Cash Basis" in the Balance Sheet report. One reader recently wrote, "I don't understand what's wrong. I run two companies and in one company the cash basis balance sheet shows A/R and A/P balances and in the other company they aren't listed. Have I done something wrong in configuring the company file that's showing these balances?"

If you are tracking inventory, and any receivables or payables involve inventory items, those transactions are included in cash-basis reports.

Month by Month P & L Reports

A reader wrote to say he was frustrated trying to design a customized report from scratch to deliver to his clients. The report he needs is a month-by-month report for the P & L. He's using the Custom Summary Report (Reports | Custom Reports | Summary) which is designed to let users create reports from scratch, but he can't figure out how to get the results he wants.

You don't have to do any work at all to get this report, because month-by-month P & L reports are built in to the standard P & L report. Getting a month-by-month P& L report is easy.

1. Choose **Reports | Company & Financial | Profit & Loss Standard** to open the report.

2. From the Dates drop down list, select the date range you need (Quarter, Year, or customized To/From dates).

3. Move to the Columns drop down list and choose **Month**.

NOTE: *The Columns drop-down list includes plenty of choices for breaking out the report numbers; you're not limited to month-by-month.*

Cash Basis Income Reports

A reader wrote to ask why creating cash basis reports seems to result in inaccurate numbers. "All invoiced amounts show on the P&L accrual report, but when I switch to cash basis, some of the paid invoices don't show up as income. Is this a user error, or is there some preference I need to change?"

We've found that when this happens, the problem is usually the date range selected for the report. For example, if you sent an invoice to a customer in September, the invoice appears in the P & L reports for the period ending September 30th. If the payment arrived in October, when you switch the report to Cash Basis, the payment won't appear unless you also switch the date range to October.

Vendor Posting Account Reports

A reader wrote to say that his boss wanted to see a list of the expense accounts for each month's vendor bills. He tried several reports in the Vendor reports section, but the posting accounts weren't displayed (he could see them when he double-clicked the "Splits" column, but he couldn't get that information to print). Here's how to get that information in a printed report:

1. Choose **Reports | Accountant & Taxes | Journal** to open the Journal report.
2. Select the appropriate date range from the Dates drop down list.
3. Click **Customize Report** (Modify Report in pre-QuickBooks 2012 versions) to open the Modify Report dialog.
4. Click the **Filters** tab to select a filter.
5. Choose **Transaction Type** in the Choose Filter list
6. From the Transaction Type drop down list, select **Bill**.

7. Click **OK** to save the new filter settings.

The report shows each bill, with columns for the credit and debit sides of the transaction. The credit side is always A/P and the debit side is the expense account(s).

If you sometimes write direct checks in addition to paying bills, filter the report for Multiple Transaction Types and select **Check** and **Bill**. (For direct checks, the credit side is a bank account instead of A/P.)

Subtotals on the P & L

An accountant wrote to ask how to get QuickBooks to subtotal groups of accounts in the P & L Report. He said that his Peachtree clients can select a range of accounts for subtotals as part of the configuration process for the P & L, but he can't find any way to select account ranges for subtotals in QuickBooks. He wants his clients' P & L reports to display subtotals for payroll expenses, sales expenses, and then the remaining expenses, followed by the grand total of expenses.

The way to do this in QuickBooks is to use subaccounts, and you must also be using numbered accounts (to eliminate the alphabetic order of accounts). Create an account named Payroll (assuming an account of that name doesn't exist). Use an account number that places the account just before the current list of payroll expense accounts. Then drag the payroll expense accounts to the right to make them subaccounts of the new parent account (or edit the payroll expense accounts to configure them as subaccounts of the parent account). Perform the same action for each group of accounts you want to subtotal.

Removing the Pennies from Reports

Many accountants "round" numbers to dollars for reports and tax returns, eliminating the decimal point and the pennies, and they want to know how to do this in QuickBooks. (Users also have asked about this, explaining that their accountants have requested reports without the pennies.)

QuickBooks reports can be configured to omit the pennies:

1. Click **Customize Report** (Modify Report in earlier QuickBooks versions) and move to the Fonts & Numbers tab.

2. Select the option labeled **Without Cents**.

3. Click **OK** to save the settings and view the report with all dollar figures rounded.

Exporting Customized Reports Created in QuickBooks Pro

Readers who use QuickBooks Pro have written to ask us how to get a report they customized in one company file into another company file instead of rebuilding the report from scratch for each company file that needs this report.

Only QuickBooks Premier editions can export report templates. All editions of QuickBooks can import report templates.

The easiest way to export your customized report is to find someone who uses a Premier edition of the same version (year) as your version. If you don't know anyone who fits that description, ask your accountant or see if your accountant might ask a Premier edition user on your behalf.

Back up the company file that contains the report to a USB flash drive and restore it on that person's computer. Save the restored file to the USB flash drive. Open the Memorized Report List and export the memorized report to the flash drive (the file is saved in the format <ReportName>.QBR).

When you get back to your own computer, open each company file that needs the report and import the report from the flash drive (you can delete the company file and the backup file that's on the flash drive).

Reporting by Customers' States

A reader wrote to say she couldn't figure out how to create a report for customers in certain states.

Unfortunately, QuickBooks doesn't "read" the state information in the customer record when you create reports. If you know you'll need reports for this information, you have a couple of choices.

You can create a Customer Type for each state.

1. Choose **Lists | Customer & Vendor Profile Lists | Customer Type List** to open the Customer Type List.

2. Press **CTRL-N** to open the New Customer Type dialog and enter the desired information.

3. Click **OK** to save the new customer type.

4. Repeat the process as needed.

If you're already using the Customer Type field for another purpose you have one more option. Use a custom field.

1. Open any customer record (custom fields created in one record appear in all records) and click the **Additional Info** tab.

2. Click the **Define Fields** button to display the Set Up Custom Fields For Names dialog.

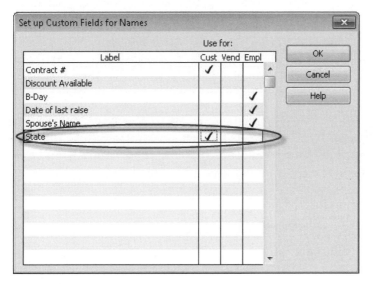

3. Enter **State** in the first blank line of the Label column.

4. Check the columns for each record type in which you want the new custom field to appear (your can have the field appear in customer, vendor, and employee records).

5. Click **OK** to save the new field, then click **OK** again to close the customer record.

6. Open each record in which you want to add data for the new custom field and enter it.

Collections Report

We periodically receive requests for help in designing a report of outstanding customer balances along with the telephone number for each customer, so users can call the customers. QuickBooks provides this information in the Collections Report (which many users don't seem to know about).

1. Choose **Reports | Customers & Receivables | Collections Report**.

2. From the Dates drop down list select the timeframe to include.

3. Use the Past Due field to set the number of days past due. For example, if you don't start to panic until a customer is 10 days past due, enter **10** in the Past Due field. The default is 1.

Memorized Report Can Be Used for Different Customers

A reader posed the following problem: "I send customers with an open balance larger than $5000.00 an open balance report. Each time I create the report I have to customize the report to add a column for the customer's purchase order number. I can't memorize the report because I may have many customers who will receive it, but I'd like to make the PO Number column appear automatically. How can I do this?"

You CAN memorize the report after you've added the PO Number column. When you need to send it to a customer, open the report and click the **Customize Report** (Modify Report in older versions) button to display the Modify Report dialog. Click the **Filters** tab and select the appropriate customer name.

Tracking Job Costs That Have Been Paid

A reader asked how to create a report that will indicate the job costs that have been paid instead of the total costs linked to the job. It's actually pretty simple.

1. Choose **Reports | Company & Financial | Profit & Loss By Job** from the menu bar.
2. Select the date range from the Dates field.
3. Click the **Customize Report** button (Modify Report in pre-2012 QuickBooks versions).
4. On the Display tab change the Report Basis to **Cash** and click **OK** to return to the report.

Viewing the Posting Details of a Transaction

We often hear from users and accountants who want to know a quick way to double- check postings. When an accountant is visiting a client site, sometimes the accountant wants to know how a particular transaction was posted to the general ledger. Most users create a report, customize it to filter for a certain account or name, and then double-click the transaction in question to drill down and see the details of the accounts listed in the column labeled "Split."

It's usually easier to find the transaction in the Customer or Vendor Center and open the original transaction window. When the transaction window is open, press **CTRL-Y** to see a posting report that includes the accounts and amounts on the Debit and Credit sides of the transaction.

CHAPTER 32:
STARTUP TIPS & TRICKS

Keep QuickBooks Running For Quick Startups.

If you select this option, QuickBooks starts when Windows starts and continues to run in the background when you close the software. The next time you want to open QuickBooks it loads immediately (because it's actually still running).

However, keeping QuickBooks running takes up RAM and other computer resources. In addition, you may have trouble updating, uninstalling, or repairing QuickBooks because software needs to be closed in order to apply changes. Before attempting those tasks, deselect this option and reboot your computer.

–Excerpt from **Running QuickBooks in Nonprofits: 2nd Edition** by Kathy Ivens (available at www.cpa911.com)

Corrupt Company Files Prevents QuickBooks from Opening

A number of readers have written in to say that QuickBooks suddenly stops opening (displays an error message during startup and won't open). Unfortunately, this is not an uncommon problem. There's a good chance it could be because the data file that was open when QuickBooks was last closed is corrupt.

Fortunately, there's an easy way to test whether this is the problem.

1. Press and hold the **CTRL** key when you double-click your QuickBooks shortcut.

2. Continue to hold the **CTRL** key until QuickBooks loads. This forces QuickBooks to start without opening a company file, and you see the No Company Open dialog with a list of previously opened files.

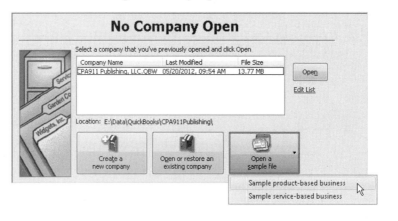

NOTE: *If QuickBooks opens, it's probable that the company file is corrupt. If it doesn't open, you have a problem with the program files, and you may need to report the error message to QuickBooks support. However, before you do, see the next tip.*

3. Try opening a sample file, and if it opens without error, you've narrowed the problem down to your company file.

4. Restore the last backup, and if that doesn't work try restoring the previous backup (you should always have at least two or three backups).

5. If nothing works, contact QuickBooks support to learn about the options for repairing your company file.

The Nuclear Option for Opening QuickBooks

After trying the previous suggestion for opening QuickBooks (hold the CTRL key until QuickBooks loads without opening a company file), several readers responded that it didn't work for them. Well, recently we ran into the same problem after a Windows 7 crash. No matter what we did, QuickBooks refused to load. Fortunately, after some painstaking research we did find a solution.

Apparently the QuickBooks DataPath key in the registry became corrupted by the crash. The solution was actually quite simple.

CAUTION: *This tip involves editing the Windows registry. If done incorrectly it can cause serious problems with not only the QuickBooks installation, but with other programs as well. Therefore, do not attempt to perform this procedure unless you are comfortable working in the Windows registry AND you backup (export) the registry first.*

If you follow these steps carefully you should be able to clear up a corrupted datapath key problem. Begin by creating a backup of the registry.

1. Go to the Windows Start menu and click **Run**.

2. Enter **regedit** and click **OK** to open the registry editor.

3. Select **File | Export** to open the Export Registry File dialog.

4. From the Save In: drop down list select a location in which to save the registry backup file.

5. In the bottom, left corner of the dialog select **ALL** from the Export Range options.

6. Enter an appropriate name in the File Name: field.

7. Click **Save** to create the backup.

Once the backup is made you're ready to edit the registry.

1. Locate the HKEY_LOCAL_MACHINE\SOFTWARE\ Wow6432Node\Intuit\QuickBooks\22.0\accountant\ DataPath key.

NOTE: We are running 64bit Windows 7 and QuickBooks Premier Accountant 2012. Depending on the version of windows and the version of QuickBooks you're using, the key will be somewhat different. For example, in Windows XP 32bit the key is HKEY_LOCAL_MACHINE\SOFTWARE\Intuit\ QuickBooks\22.0\accountant\DataPath. The 22.0 indicates this is 2012. If you're running QuickBooks 2011, the number will be 21.0 and so on.

---

2. Right-click the DataPath key and select **Modify** to open the Edit String dialog box. Do NOT delete the key.

3. Delete the contents of the Value Data: field.

4. Click **OK** to save the change.

5. Close the registry.

6. Open QuickBooks.

If QuickBooks still refuses to open it's time to call QuickBooks support.

Eliminate the QuickBooks Login Screen

A reader wrote to say, "I'm the only user of our QuickBooks software and I log in as Admin." How can I eliminate the Login window?

The QuickBooks Login window appears under either of the following circumstances:

- There is more than one user configured for the company file.
- Only the Admin user exists, and there is a password attached to the Admin account.

If you don't want to log in, follow these steps:

1. Select **Company | Set Up Users And Passwords | Set Up Users** to open the User List dialog.

2. Delete all users except Admin.

3. Select **Admin** and click the **Edit User** button.

4. Delete the existing password, leaving both the Password and Confirm Password fields blank.

5. If you have a Challenge Question, reset the drop down list to **<Select>**.

6. Click **Next**. At this point QuickBooks will suggest that you add a password. Answer **No** when asked.

7. Click **Finish**.

CAUTION: Don't do this if your computer is located where other users can get to it.

Suppressing the Saved Desktop when Logging In

A reader wrote to ask for help for one user who could no longer log in to QuickBooks - the program hung forever and finally had to be closed via Task Manager. In response to our suggestions for testing, he ascertained that this occurred only for this user's login, no matter which network computer was being used (eliminating the possibility of a damaged software installation on the user's regular computer). This user had configured QuickBooks to save the desktop when she closed QuickBooks, and her desktop usually had multiple transaction windows and customized reports open.

We're guessing that one of the reports is damaged and cannot load, and we told the reader how to force QuickBooks to let this user log in:

1. In the QuickBooks Login dialog, enter the User Name (if it isn't entered automatically) and enter the password.
2. Hold the **Alt** key while clicking **OK**. QuickBooks does not attempt to load the saved desktop.

To prevent the problem from recurring, it's a good idea to change the configuration settings to stop QuickBooks from saving all open windows when it closes.

1. Choose **Edit | Preferences** to open the Preferences dialog.
2. Click the **Desktop View** icon in the left pane and the **My Preferences** tab in the right pane.
3. In the Desktop section select the **Don't Save The Desktop** option.
4. Click **OK** to save the new setting.

Changing this option offers one additional benefit to all users, even those not experiencing start up problems. It takes more time for Quick-Books to load a saved desktop than it takes to click a few times to open the windows you need to work with after you're logged on.

CHAPTER 33:

UPDATING TIPS & TRICKS

QuickBooks provides an automatic update service you use to make sure your QuickBooks software is up-to-date and trouble-free. This service provides you with any maintenance releases of QuickBooks that have been created since you purchased and installed your copy of the software.

An update (maintenance release) is distributed when a problem is discovered and fixed. This is sometimes necessary, because it's almost impossible to distribute a program that is totally bug-free (although my experience has been that QuickBooks generally releases without any major bugs, since Intuit does a thorough job of testing its software before it's released).

The Update QuickBooks service also provides enhancements to features, along with notes from Intuit that help you keep up with new features and information about QuickBooks.

NOTE: This service does not provide upgrades to a new version; it just provides updates to your current version.

The Update QuickBooks service is an online service, so you must have set up online access in QuickBooks. To check for updates, and to configure update options choose Help | Update QuickBooks.

–Excerpt from **Running QuickBooks in Nonprofits: 2nd Edition** by Kathy Ivens (available at www.cpa911.com)

Update Options

Many users write to tell us that their accountants or computer consultants turned off the automatic update feature, and they want to know if this is dangerous or even advisable.

Here at CPA911, we don't think it's dangerous, and we even deem it advisable — we turn off automatic updates immediately after installing QuickBooks. We believe that users who have control over substantial changes to their software have less risk of problems.

(We believe the same thing about automatically updating Windows, and have our Windows update options set to ask us which updates we want to download instead of automatically updating Windows. As a result, we didn't get caught up in the problem of trying to run QuickBooks and other software that had problems after Microsoft automatically updated Internet Explorer to IE7.)

TIP: We also delete the shortcut to check for updates that appears in the Startup folder of the Programs menu when you install QuickBooks.

If you turn off automatic updates, QuickBooks periodically reminds you to check for updates when you exit QuickBooks. You can check for updates at that time, or wait until the next time you use QuickBooks.

If you're on a network, make sure that when you check for updates and find an update (and download it), all the other computers running QuickBooks are also updated.

Confusion About Shared Updates

We get quite a bit of e-mail from readers who are confused about the shared updates feature, which is a way to download an update to one computer, and then let the other computers on the network get the update from that computer. If you don't remember to enable every computer on the network for shared updates, updating can get more complicated.

When you enable shared updates, QuickBooks changes the location into which it saves the update on the computer that downloads the update (and I have never figured out why sharing the update requires that location change — there's no technical reason for this in Windows, it's purely a QuickBooks decision).

Shared updates are a convenience, not a "rule" for networked Quick-Books computers. The feature dates back to the days when users had a telephone modem on one computer, and even if the network had been set up to share that modem, the slow transfer rate of a modem made it ago-nizingly slow to update multiple computers.

The only "rule" is that all the computers on the network should be running the same version of QuickBooks in order to share data files. It doesn't matter how you deliver the update files to the computers. If all your users have access to a high-speed Internet connection, it's perfectly okay to skip the Shared Updates option and let each computer update its files manually or automatically over the Internet.

Enterprise to Pro/Premier Conversion

We have many messages from users who want to abandon Enterprise Solutions and move to Pro/Premier. However, you can't open an Enterprise File in Pro or Premier; instead you must convert your Enterprise data and import it into Pro or Premier.

These e-mails cite several reasons for moving away from Enterprise Solutions, and one of these days we may "editorialize" on this subject. However, for now we'll just say that doing this requires a conversion pro-cess.

We recommend the Enterprise-To-Pro-Or-Premier conversion services offered at q2q. Karl Irvin, the developer of q2q software, is an accom-plished expert and our clients have had excellent results with his utilities (so have we). You can download the software and perform the conversion yourself, or have q2q perform the conversion for you. More information is available at: http://www.q2q.us/EnterpriseToPro.htm

CHAPTER 34:
USERS TIPS & TRICKS

The notion of giving permissions implies the need for a person who's in charge of everyone and everything. In QuickBooks, that person is the administrator—the person with supreme power. QuickBooks uses the name Admin for the administrator.

You can set up other users with permission to access all areas of QuickBooks, which essentially makes them administrators. However, no user except the user Admin has absolute power. Only Admin can perform the following tasks:

- *Change user permissions*
- *Import and export data*
- *Change the company setup information*
- *Change company preferences*

To become the administrator, all you have to do is grab the title; the person who creates the company file and initiates the process of setting up users is de-facto the administrator. While it's preferable that the administrator is a QuickBooks expert and has some training in bookkeeping or accounting, QuickBooks presents no quiz and lets anyone become the administrator.

From a practical point of view, the important criterion is availability— an administrator should be someone who is in the office regularly so that administrative tasks can be performed when necessary.

–Excerpt from **Running QuickBooks in Nonprofits: 2nd Edition**
by Kathy Ivens (available at www.cpa911.com)

Who's Working in QuickBooks?

A reader wrote to say that occasionally he has to perform a task that requires putting QuickBooks into Single-User Mode. He asked if there's a way to find out which users are currently logged on so he can notify them of the impending change in mode.

You don't have to wander the halls peeking into every office, nor call everyone who has QuickBooks installed; just choose **Company | Set Up Users** from the menu bar. A list of all your users appears and the text "(logged on)" appears next to every user who is currently working in QuickBooks. Those are the only people you have to contact.

Can't Display User Name in QuickBooks Login Screen

Many readers have written to ask how to select a name when a user other than the last user (usually Admin) is trying to log into QuickBooks.

QuickBooks does not offer a drop-down list of user names in the Login screen, the user has to replace the currently displayed user name by typing in his/her user name.

Lost or Forgotten Closing Date Password

We frequently receive queries from users who can't remember the password they set for the Closing Date and want to make changes to a transaction in a closed period. (We're assuming the changes are minor, such as memo text, and don't affect numbers that were used in a filed tax form.)

It's easy to change the password; just delete the current password and enter a new one. You don't have to know the current password to make changes.

However, only the QuickBooks Admin can enter the password, so be sure nobody else has your Admin password.

Index